SIMPLE FRENCH BISTRO FOOD AT HOME

La Régalade

To Linda —

Bon Appétit.

Amicalement

Alain

SIMPLE FRENCH BISTRO FOOD AT HOME

La Régalade

Alain Rayé

whitecap

VANCOUVER | TORONTO

Editor: Elizabeth Wilson
Copy Editor: Ben D'Andrea
Proofreader: Marial Shea
Front Cover Designer: Jacqui Thomas
Designer: Diane Yee
Photography: Greg Blue
Illustrations: Agathe Delange
Typesetting and Rear Cover Design: Five Seventeen

Printed and bound in Canada

Library and Archives Canada Cataloguing in Publication

Rayé, Alain
          La Régalade : simple French bistro food at home / Alain Rayé.

Includes index.
ISBN 1-55285-705-0

          1. Cookery, French. I. Title.

TX719.R38 2005   641.5944   C2005-903042-9

The publisher acknowledges the financial support of the Government of
Canada through the Book Publishing Industry Development Program for
our publishing activities.

To all the people who have helped me along the way

Table of Contents

Spring

Winter

Other Recipes

Foreword

A good chef can prepare plenty of plates with skill, even panache. A great one can cook anything.

Meet one of the greats. Eat some of his food.

Chances are you already have; in the relatively short time Alain Rayé's La Régalade has been in existence—what ... four years?—thousands of locals and visitors have braved the creaky old Lions Gate Bridge into darkest West Vancouver and sat down to dinner at his bistro in the burbs. Best bistro in the burbs, and so say all of us: critics, commentators, colleagues, competitors, and all those dinner guests.

When I say a great chef can cook anything—and Alain Rayé is great among the greats—I don't mean he spreads himself thin, fuses for the sake of fusion. You won't find totteringly tall food here, or outrageous combinations that rarely even work on paper, let alone the plate. This hale and hearty cook, et sa femme, the unfailingly charming Brigitte, and no less hearty dessert-chef son, Steeve, favour food that's simple, tasty, local whenever possible (without being fanatical about it), and fresh.

"He really understands what real, local food is all about," said Canada's doyenne of food writers, Anita Stewart. We were sitting at La Régalade one evening in spring, tucking into the chef's great, simple food: stews, casseroles, braised this, and long-stewed that. Everything was in the taste—and all the flavours rang true.

Which is really what it's all about. That, and perspective. Anyone with a good eye and some colour sense, a steady hand, and a little imagination, can make designer dishes—which are often what another great, Claudio Aprile, terms "insecure food"—artfully poised pieces of vegetables, rakishly angled spears of rosemary, record-changer stacks of meat 'n' mushroom slices, all that lot. The only thing towering about Alain Rayé's cooking is the taste, which towers and often overpowers.

But in order to make country-good soul food—French or otherwise—you need heart and soul. All the rest is just technique, learnable. From a book, even. The heart and soul part is passion, and that's all from within.

These days Alain Rayé is cooking from the depths of heart and soul. And from the country. That's where he lives; so the country happens to be in Canada's most affluent postal code, West Vancouver, so what?

"This is brilliant," said Anita Stewart, as we lipsmacked our way towards the end of the meal. "He gets it!" And so do we. There aren't a lot of secrets—*trucs*—in here; mostly it's creativity, commingled with common sense, a deep respect for fresh flavours and top-flight ingredients, a love of food.

The best things are often the simplest: beef braised with carrots, potatoes gratinéed with an abundance of butter and cream; fresh, ripe tomatoes the same way; smoked herring with bay leaves and onions and boiled potatoes—what could be simpler? What could be better?

And real quantities. All right, some might say unreal quantities. There's a lot of food going down here. My advice to first-timers at La Régalade is always the same: check out the desserts, made by Steeve Rayé, which—prudently, I think—are displayed on the front counter as you come in. See which of these traditional country treats—*isles flottantes*, *Paris Brest*, *tarte*, etc.—you're going to want. And then govern yourself accordingly. That might mean no starter—none of the herring this time, or the duck confit with frisée and walnut oil—those are both meals in themselves. Go straight to the braised beef or the grilled quails with the cheese-sage polenta, or the navarin of lamb.

Yes, there are vegetables for the guilt-ridden. But in the main, this is a matter of rich, deeply flavoured country dishes, no amount of calories spared. It's the apotheosis of French country cooking in all its vast variety and resolutely fattening simplicity.

The little restaurant has become a major destination, for locals as well as visitors. Not just for the food but also for the wine. Because for a born and bred Frenchman, Alain Rayé has an uncharacteristically wide appreciation—let's come right out and call it love—for all kinds of wines, from all kinds of places, especially—glory be!—British Columbia.

Oh, sure, he delights in an obscure petit château that tastes like a hundred-dollar bottle but costs a fifth of that, but he'll also pour something extra special from the South Okanagan with a gleeful grin. That Black Hills Nota Bene for instance—amazing!

And now we can match our favourite wines with the chef's favourite recipes—so do attempt this at home. It's why you're here, why you're holding this book. The beef, the quails, the duck, the potatoes, the desserts! Just as with his in-house cooking, these recipes are simple, hearty, soul-and-palate satisfying.

Not that Alain Rayé can't or won't do complicated. My first meal at his hands came years ago, shortly after his arrival in Vancouver. It was a sensational dish of loin of lamb cooked in a cloud of hay. Yes, the kind those ruminants like to chew on. I drove all over the Fraser Valley looking for a brick-sized block of hay. Not easy to come by when you're dealing in bales the size of a Citroën C2.

But it's the simple stuff—those often less-than-stylish cuts of beef or pork or lamb; those little birds; those filling and fulfilling starches, like butter-creamed potatoes or cheese-laden polenta, or olive-oiled noodles—that really make this a cuisine to make your own. And a restaurant to return to.

I think this is the way to do it: go to La Régalade, try a few dishes, then try them according to the recipes in the book. Then go back and see how yours compared. Then do it again. Could be a decade's worth of tasty entertainment ahead.

Do visit when you're here: La Régalade may not be where the stars are—those visiting celebrities who need to be seen in order to get ink in the gossip columns—but it's most surely where the other stars are: those which, when grouped in twos or threes by the Big Red Book, *Le Guide Michelin*, bear the legend "excellent cooking, worth a detour" and "exceptional cuisine, worth a special journey."

Even on a frequently traffic-choked three-lane bridge. Pure and simple.

Here's my salute to the man with the heart and soul, the ideas and most of all the passion. Here's a toast—with a glass of, oh, let's say La Frenz Shiraz or a Joie Year One Noble Blend—to simplicity and passion. Taste and good taste.

And Chef Rayé's labours of love. About to become some of your own.

JURGEN GOTHE
FOOD & WINE EDITOR, *NUVO* MAGAZINE
AUTHOR OF *Some Acquired Tastes, Good Gothe!*
First Rate, The DiscDrive 20th Anniversary Cookbook
and *DiscCookery*
SPRING 2005, VANCOUVER, BC

Acknowledgments

MANY PEOPLE COLLABORATED in bringing this cookbook to life, and I would like to take the time to acknowledge them. Thank you, Carole Dulude, friend and newly inducted Dame d'Escoffier, for your great help in translating my recipes and thoughts. Thank you, Agathe Delange, for your talent and joyful illustrations, amusing us through the seasons. Thank you, Greg Blue, for your stunning photography portraying La Régalade dishes and their French spirit. Thank you, Jurgen Gothe, for your kind words and your love of French cuisine.

Above all, La Régalade is a family affair. I thank my wife, Brigitte, profoundly, for her hard work and for being at my side for all of those years in this demanding business. I thank my son Steeve for his collaboration and great culinary instincts. Thank you also, Kevin, for your kindness and understanding.

Last but not least, thanks to you, guests and friends, for honouring us with your visits and your praise. La Régalade wouldn't exist without you!

Introduction

COOKING IS THE HAPPINESS OF MY LIFE. This is my art, my way of communicating, and my true passion. As any artist knows, the joy of creating is surpassed only by the joy of sharing your creations. Sharing my cuisine with people who appreciate food is my ultimate satisfaction.

La Régalade—meaning "a succulent treat"—was the perfect venue to share simple but traditional comforting bistro fare. Bistro cuisine is the closest you can come to a real, down-to-earth French culinary experience. Fresh regional ingredients, cooked slowly with love and attention, shared humbly between family and friends are what we're all about.

With this cookbook, you can be the great French chef in your family, recreating the same authentic and delicious bistro dishes that you find on our blackboards every day, and sharing great French food, joviality, and hospitality in your own home.

Don't forget to kiss your guests on each cheek when they arrive! A tradition is a tradition. Bonne chance et bon appétit!

ALAIN RAYÉ

Spring

AS A CULINARY PROFESSIONAL, I always saw the arrival in town of the *marchés nouveaux* as the first sign that spring had arrived. I'd arrive early at the town's farmers' market to buy the first lettuces of the season, the first fresh herbs, and baby vegetables. Artichokes, asparagus, spinach, and the other tender vegetables of the season need only to be simply steamed, lightly coated, or delicately seasoned to abound in goodness.

Spring in France also means Easter celebrations. On Easter Sunday, the traditional dish is *l'agneau pascal*—Easter lamb. The very best came from Lozère, where the lambs graze on a thin row of greenery between Mont Saint-Michel and the sea, and their flesh is naturally salted. Delicious. After a copious lunch, the children would go in the garden to find their chocolate treats. Where Brigitte comes from in Burgundy, the children would run after Easter eggs that were rolled down steep hills.

The slow-cooked onions and the scallops meld their sweetness to make a satisfying dish that, to me, is very feminine. This dish is good with a simple green salad. If you wish to give the tart a bit of an edge, add a spoonful of Beluga caviar on top of each serving.

Onion Tarts with Scallop Carpaccio

TARTELETTES À L'OIGNON, CARPACCIO DE ST-JACQUES

1 sheet frozen puff pastry
(thaw according to package directions)

1 Tbsp (15 mL) olive oil

1 large onion, chopped

Salt and pepper

1 sprig thyme

16 sea scallops (partially frozen)

Preparation time: 30 minutes
Cooking time: 11 minutes
Serves 4

CUT FOUR 6-inch (15-cm) circles from the puff pastry, using a bowl or cutter.

Preheat the oven to 280°F (145°C).

Heat the olive oil in large frying pan. Add the onion and season with salt, pepper, and thyme; sauté until soft, but not brown. Top each puff pastry circle with a thin layer of onion and bake in the oven for about 10 minutes.

Slice the partially frozen scallops thinly and place the slices in circles on parchment paper cut into 8-inch (20-cm) rounds (a bit larger than the puff pastry circles). Brush the scallops with olive oil. When the pastry is baked, delicately flip each circle of scallops onto the pastry. Put the tarts back in the oven for just 30 seconds, to warm up the scallops. Season with sea salt (Guerande salt), if desired, and serve with a green salad.

(For a change, mix the onion with cooked and drained diced bacon.)

SUGGESTED WINES
Chablis 1er Cru, Domaine Laroche, France
or Chardonnay Reserve, Mission Hills, BC

This recipe is based on earthy cuisine, as one might guess from the unglamorous name. I love the way the pork fat gives the soup a velvety texture. You can substitute fava beans for the peas and add one sprig of rosemary for a different flavour.

Pea and Lard Soup

SOUPE DE PETITS POIS AU LARD

1 large onion

1 medium carrot

¼ lb (125 g) unsmoked bacon

2 Tbsp (30 mL) canola oil

1 lb (500 g) fresh green peas, shells removed

8 cups (2 L) milk

Salt and pepper

Pinch sugar

½ cup (125 mL) unsalted butter

¼ cup (60 mL) whipping cream

2 sprigs chervil

Preparation time: 30 minutes
Cooking time: 15 minutes
Serves 6

PEEL, WASH, AND MINCE the onion and carrot. Cut the bacon into cubes.

Sweat the bacon and vegetables gently in the oil in a heavy-bottomed pot until the onions are transparent. Add the peas and add just enough milk to cover the vegetables. Season with salt, pepper, and a pinch of sugar. Simmer for 15 minutes or until the peas are soft but still bright green.

Blend the soup in a food processor and add the butter a bit at a time. Add the cream and pass through a sieve. Serve warm in soup plates garnished with chervil.

SUGGESTED WINES
Pinot Gris d'Ostertag, France
or Pinot Gris, Poplar Grove, BC

This is rich and best consumed in moderation, but the combination of chicken liver and foie gras served on crostini is the perfect gourmand's food.

Chicken Liver Mousse

MOUSSE DE FOIES DE VOLAILLE

2 Tbsp (30 mL) unsalted butter

10 chicken livers

5 oz (150 g) fresh foie gras

Salt and pepper

1 Tbsp (15 mL) cognac

1 Tbsp (15 mL) port

⅔ cup (160 mL) whipping cream

Preparation time: 45 minutes
Cooking time: 15 minutes
Resting time: 5 to 6 hours
Serves 4

HEAT A HEAVY-BOTTOMED PAN over medium heat, melt the butter, and cook the livers for a few minutes without browning. They should be just a bit past the pink stage. Cut the cooked liver into pieces, season with salt and pepper and set aside in a food processor to cool slightly. Pour the fat out of the pan and return to high heat. Add cognac and port to the pan, scraping off any pieces of cooked liver, and bring to a boil. Add the liquid to the livers in the food processor. Add the cream and blend until completely smooth.

Check the seasoning, pour the mixture into a 4-inch (10-cm) terrine, wrap, and refrigerate for 5 to 6 hours. Serve directly from the terrine with slices of toasted country bread and a lamb's lettuce or mesclun salad with a nut-oil-based vinaigrette.

SUGGESTED WINES
Vouvray Demi-Sec, Domaine Champalou, France
or Viognier, Jackson Triggs, BC

I like the contrast between the bitterness of lemons and the sweetness of mussels. It makes a great appetizer because, even if you aren't hungry, after a few bites, you want to eat more!

Mushroom and Mussel Salad
SALADE DE CHAMPIGNONS ET MOULES

2 lb (1 kg) mussels

1 lb (500 g) small white button mushrooms (cut in half if large)

4 tsp (20 mL) lemon juice

2 large tomatoes

1 tsp (5 mL) olive oil

3 red shallots, finely chopped

1 cup (250 mL) cider vinegar

1 lemon, peeled, thinly sliced and seeded

1 clove garlic, crushed and chopped

2 Tbsp (30 mL) chopped parsley

Salt and pepper

Preparation time: 35 minutes
Cooking time: 10 minutes
Serves 4

CLEAN AND SCRUB THE MUSSELS. Set aside. Clean the mushrooms and sprinkle with lemon juice. Drop the tomatoes whole in boiling water for 10 seconds. Peel, seed, and cut in quarters.

Heat the oil in a large, heavy-bottomed pot over medium heat. Add the shallots and sauté until soft. Add the tomatoes and sauté 3 more minutes while stirring constantly. Add the vinegar and mushrooms and cover. Keep to a simmer at low heat; add the lemon slices, garlic, and 1 Tbsp (15 mL) of the chopped parsley to the mixture. Season with salt and pepper and simmer 10 more minutes.

Place the mussels in the hot pot; cover for a few minutes until they open. With a slotted spoon, remove the mussels to a large bowl and cover to keep warm. With the same slotted spoon, remove the vegetables, setting aside. Heat the remaining liquid quickly and reduce before returning the vegetables and mussels and adding the remaining 1 Tbsp (15 mL) of parsley to the pot. Serve in 4 large soup plates. You can serve this dish hot or cold.

SUGGESTED WINES
Entre Deux Mers, Château Bonnet, France
or Alibi, Black Hills, BC

This recipe is a tribute to my Belgian friends: moules marinières with a side of golden french fries and a glass of good beer, as the Belgians serve it. This dish can make us think Belgium is the centre of the universe!

Mussels with White Wine and Herbs

MOULES MARINIÈRES

2 lb (1 kg) mussels
(PEI or Spring Island)

½ cup (125 mL) unsalted butter

1 onion, diced

3 Tbsp (45 mL) whipping cream

1 cup (250 mL) dry white wine

1 Tbsp (15 mL) finely chopped
flat-leaf parsley

Freshly ground black pepper

Preparation time: 15 minutes
Cooking time: 10 minutes
Serves 4

CLEAN THE MUSSELS, ensuring that beards are removed, and rinse under cold water.

In a large, heavy-bottomed pot, add the butter and onion, then the mussels, cream, wine, and parsley. Cover the pot and turn the heat to high allowing the mussels to open as quickly as possible. After about 3 minutes, stir to allow all mussels to cook. As soon as all mussels are open, season generously with freshly ground black pepper. Transfer to serving bowls and sprinkle with more parsley. Serve immediately.

SUGGESTED WINES
Bordeaux Blanc, Clos de la Floridene, France
or Allison Ranch Unoaked Chardonnay, Quails' Gate, BC

Salade Régalade

SALADE RÉGALADE

Vinaigrette

2 egg yolks

¼ cup (60 mL) Dijon mustard

2 cups (500 mL) olive oil

⅔ cup (160 mL) lobster stock
(specialty markets)

⅓ cup (80 mL) lemon juice
(about 2 lemons)

1 sprig tarragon

1 clove garlic

¼ cup (60 mL) freshly grated
Parmesan cheese

2 anchovy fillets

Dash of Tabasco

Salt and white pepper to taste

I love Caesar salads. My version uses baby romaine and warm seafood. The lemon is very important: it excites the palate, making it more receptive to other flavours.

VINAIGRETTE

COMBINE ALL THE VINAIGRETTE INGREDIENTS in a blender and pulse until they emulsify. This dressing will keep for up to a week in an airtight container in the refrigerator.

SALAD

Preheat a pan over high heat and add the oil. Sauté the prawns for about 3 minutes and remove from the pan. In the same hot pan, sauté the onion, calamari, and bacon together. At the last minute, add the tomato and green onion and season with salt and a pinch of piment d'Espelette.

In a bowl, mix the baby romaine with 5 Tbsp (75 mL) of the vinaigrette and toss loosely with large spoons. Add the warm seafood and toss well.

Serve warm in individual serving bowls, and garnish with croutons, lemon wedges, and Parmesan.

SUGGESTED WINES
Vieille Ferme Blanche, France
or Chardonnay, Township 7, BC

Salad

1 Tbsp (15 mL) olive oil

10 prawns, shelled, deveined,
and uncooked

¼ cup (60 mL) minced onion

15 small calamari,
cleaned and left whole

¼ cup (60 mL) diced bacon,
cooked and drained

¼ cup (60 mL) diced tomato

1 Tbsp (15 mL) chopped green onion

Sea salt

Pinch piment d'Espelette
(fine grocery stores)
or sweet Hungarian paprika

10 heads of baby romaine lettuce

Garnish

Croutons

Lemon wedges

Freshly grated Parmesan cheese

Preparation time: 30 minutes
Cooking time: 12 minutes
Serves 5

In France, the best, highest quality chickens come from Bresse, where breeders meet strict regulations for raising the birds, including how they're fed. Since this recipe is based on a traditional Bresse dish, choose a nice organic chicken, which will stand up well to braising and taste better.

Creamy Chicken Fricassée

FRICASSÉE DE VOLAILLE À LA CRÈME

1 large free-range chicken

All-purpose flour

½ cup (125 mL) unsalted butter

3 Tbsp (45 mL) canola oil

Salt and pepper

1 onion, peeled, washed, and cut into quarters

½ lb (250 g) white mushrooms, washed and cut in quarters

2 cloves garlic, crushed

3 Tbsp (45 mL) white wine

4 cups (1 L) whipping cream

1 bouquet garni (see page 138)

3 Tbsp (45 mL) lemon juice

Preparation time: 20 minutes
Cooking time: 45 minutes
Serves 4

ASK YOUR BUTCHER to cut the chicken into 8 pieces. Flour the chicken pieces lightly. Heat the butter and oil in a heavy-bottomed pot on high heat. Sear the chicken pieces on all sides and season with salt and pepper. Remove the pieces and set aside. Sauté the onion quarters, mushrooms, and garlic. Reduce the heat, return the chicken, and continue cooking the pieces another 5 minutes on each side. Pour in the white wine and scrape the bottom to loosen any browned bits. Reduce the heat again and add the cream and bouquet garni. Simmer, covered, for 25 to 30 minutes.

Place the chicken pieces in a serving dish. With a slotted spoon remove the bouquet garni and onion quarters from the sauce. Add the lemon juice, correct the seasoning, and bring to a boil. Pour the sauce over the chicken and serve hot. Accompany this dish with rice pilaf (see page 139).

SUGGESTED WINES
Meursault Domaine des Comtes Laffon, France
or Reserve Chardonnay, Mission Hills, BC

The spices and dried fruits give out all of their flavour in this slow-cooking dish. When I eat it, I travel in my mind to all the countries surrounding the Mediterranean. It goes beautifully with couscous.

Lamb Ragoût with Pistachios and Dried Apricots

NAVARIN D'AGNEAU AUX PISTACHES ET ABRICOTS SECS

3 lb (1.5 kg) lamb shoulder, deboned and cut into 2-inch (5-cm) cubes

Salt and pepper

¼ cup (60 mL) canola oil

2 Tbsp (30 mL) olive oil

3 onions, finely chopped

3 Tbsp (45 mL) liquid honey

2 tsp (10 mL) saffron

2 tsp (10 mL) ground ginger

2 tsp (10 mL) ground cinnamon

4 cups (1 L) water

1 lb (500 g) dried apricots

½ cup (125 mL) shelled pistachios

One 12-oz (340-g) box couscous (optional)

Extra virgin olive oil

1 small bunch fresh cilantro, chopped

Preparation time: 20 minutes
Cooking time: 45 minutes
Serves 6

SEASON THE MEAT with salt and pepper. In a deep, heavy-bottomed pot, heat the canola oil and brown the meat. Remove and set aside.

Reduce the heat, add the olive oil, and sauté the onions until soft. Return the cooked meat to the pot. Add the honey, saffron, ginger, and cinnamon. Pour in the water and add the dried apricots. Cover and simmer for 35 minutes. Add the pistachios, cover and simmer for a further 10 minutes.

Prepare couscous according to package directions. When cooked, drizzle with extra virgin olive oil and fluff with a fork. Divide among the plates. Serve the ragoût on top, sprinkled with freshly chopped cilantro.

SUGGESTED WINES
Tavel Château d'Aqueria, France
or Jackson Triggs Proprietor's Reserve Blanc de Noir, BC

This satisfying, succulent, and copious dish makes the most of spring, with young, tender lamb and fresh vegetables.

Ragoût of Lamb with Spring Vegetables

NAVARIN D'AGNEAU PRINTANIER

⅓ cup (80 mL) canola oil

7 lb (3.15 kg) boneless lamb shoulder,
cut into 1½-inch (4-cm) pieces

1 cup (250 mL) carrots,
cut in 1-inch (2.5-cm) pieces

1 cup (250 mL) onions,
cut in 1-inch (2.5-cm) cubes

½ cup (125 mL) all-purpose flour

2 Tbsp (30 mL) tomato paste

1 bouquet garni (see page 138)

Salt and pepper

4 cloves garlic, peeled and crushed

Garnish

4 large potatoes

16 baby carrots

16 baby turnips

Handful green beans

1 cup (250 mL) frozen green peas

2 Tbsp (45 mL) chopped parsley

Preparation time: 1 hour
Cooking time: 1 hour
Serves 8

PREHEAT THE BROILER.

Heat half the oil in a frying pan and sear the lamb cubes on all sides until browned. Set aside.

In a Dutch oven, heat the remaining oil, add the carrots and onions, and sweat at low heat for 5 minutes. Add the lamb to the vegetables, gently skim off the fat, and sprinkle with flour. Place under the broiler for a few minutes until the flour is brown. Remove from the oven and set the oven temperature at 400°F (200°C). Mix in the tomato paste with a wooden spoon; add the bouquet garni and season with salt and pepper. Add water to cover the meat, cover, and cook for 40 to 45 minutes depending on the quality of the meat. (The tougher the meat the longer it needs to cook).

GARNISH

Meanwhile, peel and wash the potatoes, carrots, and turnips for the garnish. Cut the vegetables and the green beans into sticks 1½ x ½ inches (4 cm x 1 cm). Blanch each vegetable separately in boiling salted water for about 5 minutes, until tender but still crisp. Bring the frozen peas to a boil and drain. Ten minutes before the lamb is cooked, add the garnish vegetables to the ragoût so that they absorb the sauce. Place the lamb on a serving dish and spoon the vegetables on and around the lamb. Pour the sauce on top and sprinkle with chopped parsley.

SUGGESTED WINES
Anjou Villages Château De Fesles, France
or Cabernet Franc, Fairview Cellars, BC

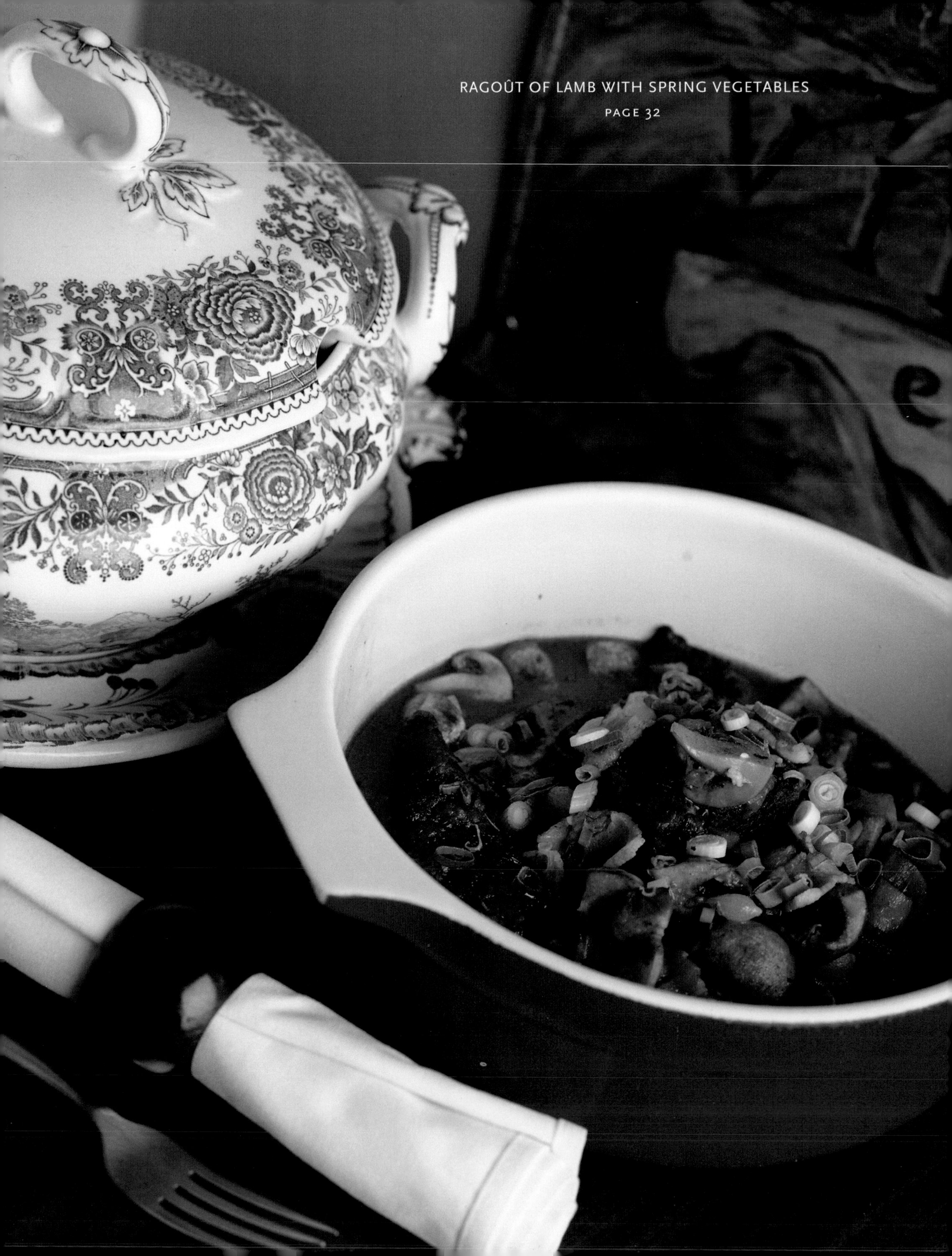

RAGOÛT OF LAMB WITH SPRING VEGETABLES

PAGE 32

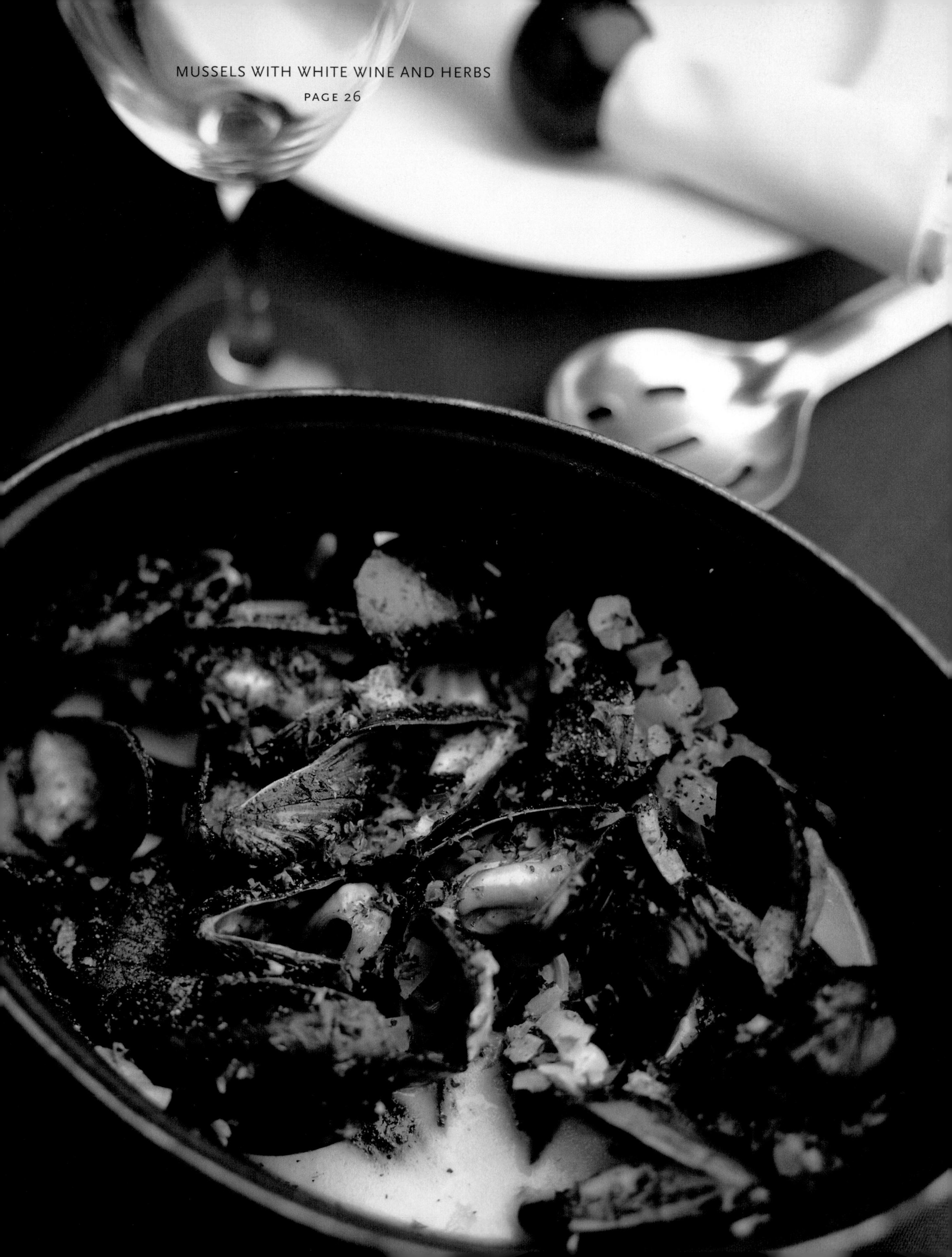

MUSSELS WITH WHITE WINE AND HERBS

PAGE 26

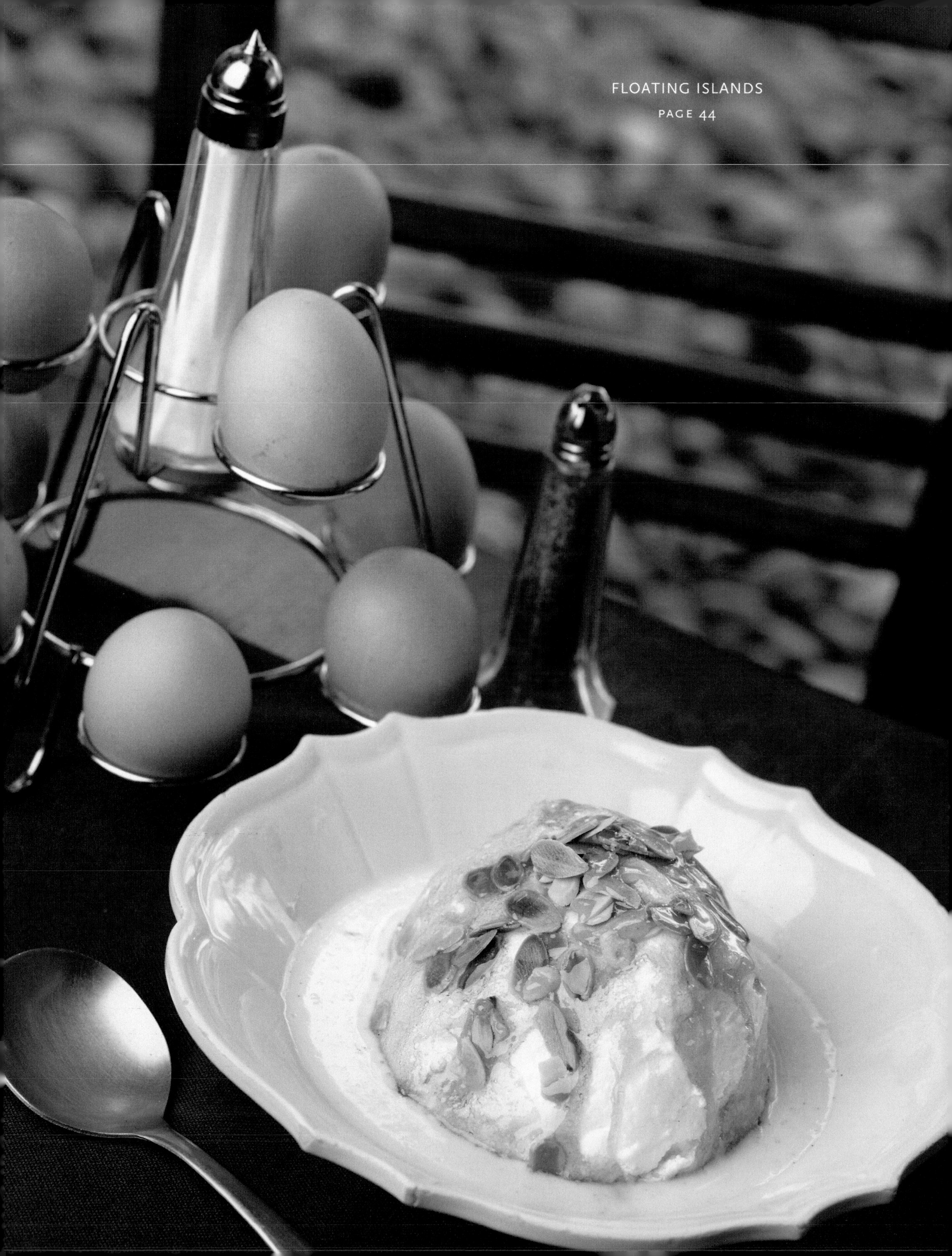

FLOATING ISLANDS

PAGE 44

OMELET WITH MARINATED MUSHROOMS

PAGE 74

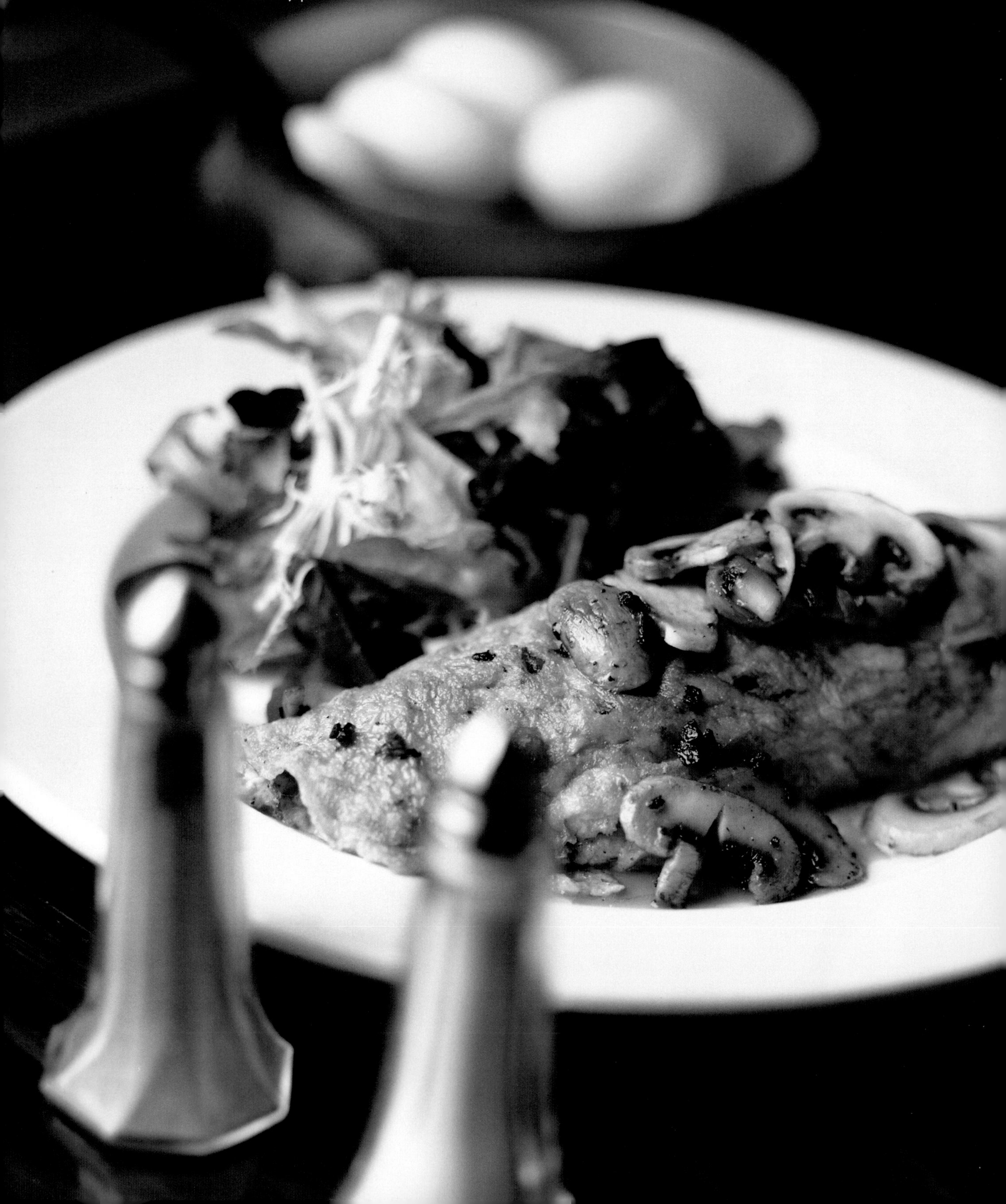

There's great harmony between the melting texture of the brisket and the carrots, as they soak up all the flavour of the beef jus. Try this dish with Dijon mustard; it's truly delicious!

Braised Beef with Carrots

BOEUF BRAISÉ AVEC CAROTTES

4–5 lb (2–2.2 kg) beef brisket

Salt and pepper

1 sprig thyme, chopped

2 fresh bay leaves

½ cup (125 mL) brandy

3 cups (750 mL) white wine

2 veal feet (ask your butcher)

½ lb (250 g) pork skin
(optional—ask your butcher)

5 cups (1.25 L) veal stock
(fine grocery stores)

¼ cup (60 mL) unsalted butter

¼ cup (60 mL) canola oil

2 Tbsp (30 mL) tomato paste

1 medium carrot,
cut into 1-inch (2.5-cm) pieces

1 medium onion,
cut into 1-inch (2.5-cm) pieces

2 Tbsp (30 mL) chopped parsley

5 cloves garlic, peeled and crushed

1 lb (500 g) carrots

50 peeled pearl onions

Chopped parsley, for garnish

Preparation time: 5 hours
Cooking time: 3 hours
Serves 6

REMOVE EXCESS FAT from the brisket. Season with salt, pepper, a pinch of the chopped thyme, and part of one of the bay leaves, finely chopped. Put the meat in a deep bowl with the brandy and white wine. The liquid must cover all of the meat. Marinate for 5 hours, flipping the meat from time to time. After 5 hours, remove the meat from the marinade, sponge with a clean cloth, and set the marinade aside in the refrigerator.

Blanch the veal feet and the pork skin in boiling water for about 10 minutes and let cool. Meanwhile, warm up the veal stock in a small pot and preheat the oven to 300°F (150°C).

Bring a frying pan to high heat, add half the butter and half the oil, and sear the brisket on each side until well browned. Transfer the brisket to a large ovenproof dish and add the tomato paste. Add the chopped carrot and onion to the frying pan, sauté lightly, and transfer to the same dish. Add the veal feet, pork skin, parsley, garlic, warm veal stock, reserved marinade, and the remaining thyme and bay leaf. Bring to a boil on the stove and bake in the oven for 2½ hours.

While the meat is cooking, cut the 1 lb (500 g) of carrots in large sticks. Blanch in boiling water for 10 minutes. Heat the remaining oil and butter in a pan over medium-high heat. Add the carrots and cook until slightly browned. Remove from the pan and set aside. Add the pearl onions to the same pan, season with salt and pepper, and cook until they are golden brown. Set aside.

After 1½ hours of cooking, take the veal feet out of the dish, discard the bones, and cut the meat into ½-inch (1-cm) cubes. Return the veal meat in with the brisket, add the carrots and pearl onion, and return to the oven for 1 hour more.

Transfer to a serving dish, with the meat in the centre and vegetables around. Pour the sauce over and garnish with chopped parsley.

SUGGESTED WINES
Pinot Noir d'Alsace Hugel, France
or Pinot Nero, D'Asolo, BC

The vermouth and curry really bring out the flavour of the clams.
Don't forget the best part: dipping your bread in the sauce.

Clams in Dry Vermouth and Curry Broth

PALOURDES AU NOILLY PRAT ET CURRY

3 lb (1.5 kg) clams

1 onion, diced

1 cup (250 mL) dry white vermouth
(Noilly Prat preferred)

Pinch curry powder

½ cup (125 mL) whipping cream

Pepper

2 Tbsp (30 mL) finely chopped parsley,
plus more for garnish

Preparation time: 15 minutes
Cooking time: 10 minutes
Serves 4

CLEAN AND WASH the clams. Place them in a heavy-bottomed pan with all the remaining ingredients. Cover the pan and cook the clams for about 7 minutes until they all open. Serve in a deep bowl and garnish with chopped parsley.

SUGGESTED WINES
Muscadet Château de la Preuille, France
or Sauvignon Blanc, Mission Hills, BC

You can tell good-quality pork by its light pink colour, dense structure, and dry surface. Pork is the best meat to bring a sweet flavour to a meat dish. With oranges, kumquats, spices, and honey, this dish may transport you to the Middle East.

Pork Shanks with Ginger and Kumquats

JARRETS DE PORC AU GINGEMBRE ET KUMQUATS

2 pork shanks

¼ cup (60 mL) canola oil

1 large onion, peeled and chopped

2 carrots, peeled and chopped

1 lb (500 g) kumquats, cut in halves

1 sprig thyme

2 bay leaves

¾ cup (180 mL) freshly squeezed orange juice (about 4 oranges)

⅓ cup (80 mL) lemon juice (about 2 lemons)

Small piece ginger root, peeled and grated

1 cinnamon stick

Salt and pepper

¼ cup (60 mL) liquid honey

½ cup (125 mL) white wine vinegar

8 whole cloves

Preparation time: 35 minutes
Cooking time: 2 hours
Serves 4

RINSE THE SHANKS, then drop into a large pot of boiling water and blanch for 8 minutes. Drain, dry, and set aside.

Preheat the oven to 350°F (180°C).

In a Dutch oven, heat the oil and sear the meat. Set aside. Sauté the vegetables in the same pot, but don't brown them. Add a quarter of the kumquat halves, plus the thyme, bay leaves, citrus juices, grated ginger, and cinnamon stick. Return meat to the pot and season with salt and pepper. Cover and cook in the preheated oven for 2 hours.

Half an hour before the meat is cooked, in a medium, heavy-bottomed pot, mix the remaining kumquats with the honey, wine vinegar, and cloves. Cook for 30 minutes over medium heat and set aside, keeping warm.

When the meat is cooked, pour the cooking juices through a sieve into a sauce dish. Arrange the meat on a serving platter and garnish with the kumquat mixture.

SUGGESTED WINES
Jurancon Clos Uroulat, France
or Kerner Late Harvest, Gray Monk, BC

Braised Veal

BLANQUETTE DE VEAU

4 lb (2 kg) veal shoulder,
cut into large cubes

3 medium carrots

¼ celery stalk

3 medium onions

2 whole cloves

2 leeks, white parts only

A few sprigs parsley

2 cloves garlic, peeled and whole

2 bay leaves

1 bouquet garni (see page 138)

1 sprig thyme

Ask your butcher to cut the veal shoulder into 2-inch (5-cm) cubes. If possible, buy milk-fed veal, which should be firm, fine-grained, and pinkish-white—all signs of excellent veal meat. For a different flavour, finely chop fresh herbs such as parsley, basil, chervil, or mint and scatter over each serving. They add a subtle but tasty finish to the dish.

PLACE THE VEAL CUBES in a large pot and cover with cold water. Bring to a boil and blanch for 3 to 4 minutes, skimming off any fat from the surface, then drain and rinse under cold water to cool.

Cut the carrots and celery into large sticks. Quarter 2 of the onions and prick the heel of the remaining onion with 2 cloves. Slice the leek whites lengthwise. Add parsley sprigs and the garlic. Place the vegetables in a tall, heavy-bottomed pot. Cover with cold water to about 1 inch (2 to 3 cm) above the meat with the parsley and garlic. Add bay leaves, bouquet garni, and thyme. Bring to a boil, then lower the heat and let simmer for 45 to 55 minutes, uncovered. Cooking time will depend on the quality of the meat. (The tougher the meat, the longer it needs to cook.)

For the sauce, melt ½ cup (125 mL) of butter in a medium pot and whisk in the flour all at once. Stirring constantly, cook mixture 3 to 4 minutes. Before it begins to colour, remove from the heat and let cool.

Peel, wash, and slice the mushrooms. In another pan, add the mushrooms and pearl onions to just enough boiling salted water to cover. Add 2 Tbsp (30 mL) butter and the lemon juice. Cook until there is no liquid left and the onions are glazed. Set aside.

Verify that the meat is tender; drain using a slotted spoon, and transfer to a covered ceramic serving dish—or a cast-iron pot for a more rustic look.

Strain the cooking liquid through a sieve and pour 4 cups (1 L) of it over the flour and butter mixture. Add a third of the mushrooms and pearl onions to the sauce and bring to a boil while constantly whisking the mixture. Cook at a low heat for 10 to 15 minutes.

Mix the egg yolks and cream in a small bowl. When the sauce has cooked, remove it from the heat and progressively whisk the cream mixture into it. Return the sauce to a boil for a few seconds. Check smoothness and seasoning.

Pour the sauce over the meat and place the remaining mushrooms and pearl onions on top. Serve with Rice Pilaf (page 139).

SUGGESTED WINES
Sancerre Rouge, Alphonse Mellot, France
or Pinot Noir, Hester Creek, BC

Sauce

½ cup (125 mL) unsalted butter

½ cup (125 mL) all-purpose flour

½ lb (250 g) small white mushrooms

20 peeled pearl onions

2 Tbsp (30 mL) unsalted butter

3 Tbsp (45 mL) lemon juice

2 egg yolks

¾ cup (180 mL) whipping cream

Salt and pepper

Preparation time: 1 hour
Cooking time: 45 to 55 minutes
Serves 6 to 8

THAT HAD BETTER BE
BEEF STEW !!!

If you want to have success with gnocchi, you'll need time to practise your technique. The potatoes make the gnocchi soft and tender and the flour allows you to shape them. After that, the skilled gnocchi maker will know how many eggs to add, depending on the texture of the potatoes and flour, or even on the humidity. To be a good cook, you need spirit, understanding, and the ability to change a recipe if needed—not always following it as I tell you!

Potato Gnocchi with Mushrooms, Prosciutto, and Romaine Ribs

GNOCCHI DE POMMES DE TERRE AUX CHAMPIGNONS,
JAMBON DE PAYS, ET CÔTES DE ROMAINE

Gnocchi

2 lb (1 kg) Yukon Gold potatoes,
skins on

2 lb (1 kg) unrefined
large-grain sea salt

1 cup (250 mL) all-purpose flour

2 egg yolks

½ cup (125 mL) grated
Parmesan cheese

Sea salt

White pepper

Olive oil for sautéing

GNOCCHI

PREHEAT THE OVEN to 325°F (160°C).

Wash and dry the potatoes. In an ovenproof dish, make a bed of sea salt and arrange potatoes on top. Bake until the flesh no longer resists the blade of a knife—around 30 to 35 minutes.

While the potatoes are hot, peel them, put into a large bowl, and immediately mash. With a wooden spoon, fold in the flour and egg yolks. Knead with your hands to obtain a smooth and homogenous texture. Add the Parmesan and knead some more. Divide the dough into 4 and roll out on a floured surface until you have formed even logs of 12 to 16 inches (30 to 40 cm). Cut with a sharp knife into 1½-inch (4-cm) pieces.

Finish rolling with the gentle push of the back of a fork, to indent the dough. Poach the gnocchi in a large pot of simmering water. Drain and salt them as they rise to the surface. Set aside in a bowl with ice-cold water.

GARNISH

Clean the chanterelles and cut in 3 or 4 pieces depending on size. Heat 1 Tbsp (15 mL) of the olive oil and 1½ tsp (7 mL) of the butter in a pan over medium-high heat. Sauté the chanterelles and shallots until soft. Season with white pepper and set aside on a plate.

Rinse and dry the romaine leaves and separate the tender ribs. (Retain the green leafy parts for another purpose.) Chop the ribs into 1½-inch (4-cm) pieces. Raise the heat to high and sauté the chopped romaine stems in the remaining butter for 2 minutes, then set aside. Cut each prosciutto slice into 3 or 4 small triangles, sauté each side, and pat dry.

Preheat the broiler.

Reduce the heat and add some olive oil. Sauté the gnocchi, but don't allow them to colour. Glaze the gnocchi with the chicken stock and add the garnish. Sauté for 1 or 2 minutes more. Place the gnocchi and garnish in a baking dish, sprinkle with the Parmesan and remaining 1 Tbsp (15 mL) olive oil, then place under the broiler for a few minutes, until the surface becomes crispy.

SUGGESTED WINES

Beaujolais Nouveau Domaine des Terres Dorées, France
or Gamay Noir, Blue Mountain, BC

Garnish

2 handfuls chanterelle mushrooms

2 Tbsp (30 mL) olive oil

1 Tbsp (15 mL) unsalted butter

2 red shallots,
peeled and chopped finely

White pepper

8 wide romaine leaves

4 thick slices prosciutto

⅔ cup (160 mL) concentrated chicken stock,
or 1 ⅓ cups chicken stock reduced by half

¼ cup (60 mL) grated parmesan cheese

Preparation time: 1½ hours
Cooking time: 20 minutes
Serves 4

To make good mashed potatoes, use well-salted water for boiling. Use 2 Tbsp (30 mL) of salt for 10 cups (2.5 L) of water and you won't have to salt again after cooking. For the smoothest and most velvety mashed potatoes, I recommend a hand-cranked food mill. Don't use a food processor. It will turn the potatoes to glue. Mashed potatoes don't keep warm, creamy, and smooth for long, so serve immediately and don't reheat.

Mashed Potatoes

PURÉE DE POMMES DE TERRE

2 lb (1 kg) Yukon Gold potatoes, skins on (about 10 medium potatoes)

1 cup (250 mL) whole milk

½ lb (250 g) butter, cut in cubes

Sea salt

Preparation time: 30 minutes
Cooking time: 45 minutes
Serves 5

PLACE THE POTATOES in a large pot and cover them with cold salted water. Bring to a boil and cook at a medium boil for 35 minutes. Meanwhile, preheat the oven to 325°F (160°C).

Use the tip of a knife to check doneness, then drain, and slip or peel the skin off while the potatoes are still hot. Place them in a shallow baking dish in the preheated oven for 3 minutes until dry. In a small pan or in the microwave, bring the milk to a boil. Return the potatoes to the large pot and mash. Add the butter all at once and whip with a wooden spoon. Mix the hot milk into the potatoes a little at a time. Beat the purée with a wooden spoon or with a hand mixer at medium speed until it is smooth and firm.

SUGGESTED WINES
Menetou Salon Georges Chavet et Fils, France
or Pinot Noir, Quails' Gate, BC

This recipe is a bit like a crème caramel, but it's flavoured with lemon. It's a very nice spring dessert, especially when served with red berries.

Upside-Down Lemon Custard

Crème renversée au citron

1 organic lemon

4 cups (1 L) 2% milk

6 eggs

¾ cup (180 mL) sugar

10 sugar cubes (for the caramel)

Preparation time: 15 minutes
Cooking time: 1 hour
Resting time: 6 hours
(overnight preferred)
Serves 5

BRUSH THE LEMON under running water, remove the zest with a peeler, and cut finely. In a saucepan, bring the milk and zest to a boil.

In a large bowl, beat the eggs and sugar until the mixture whitens. Pour the boiling milk through a sieve into the egg mixture and mix. Keep the zest aside.

Preheat the oven to 350°F (180°C).

Place the sugar cubes in a small pot with a few drops of water. On low heat, melt the sugar to make caramel. When the caramel is golden brown, pour it into a 7-inch (18-cm) soufflé dish, distributing it evenly over the bottom.

Pour in the custard mixture and stir in the reserved lemon zest. Place the soufflé dish in a larger ovenproof dish. Add water so that it comes halfway up the sides of the soufflé dish. Cook the custard in the bain-marie for 1 hour.

Remove the custard from the oven and allow it to come to room temperature before storing in the refrigerator for at least 6 hours (overnight is better). Before serving, run a knife around the edges and invert the mould onto a deep dish. Garnish with berries if desired.

SUGGESTED WINES
Muscat de Rivesaltes Domaine de Rolland, France
or Botrytis Affected Optima, Quails' Gate, BC

There are so many different crème brûlée recipes, and so many flavours. However, maybe because I'm traditional, I like my crème brûlée made with fresh vanilla beans from Tahiti. They have more flavour and more seeds inside. For a true crème brûlée, the custard should be only as thick as your thumb so that you get the crunchy top and the creamy bottom with every spoonful.

Crème Brûlée

CRÈME BRÛLÉE

3 vanilla beans

7 egg yolks

¾ cup (180 mL) sugar

1 cup (250 mL) milk

3 cups (750 mL) whipping cream

Sugar to caramelize

Preparation time: 20 minutes
Cooking time: 45 minutes
Resting time: 2 to 3 hours
Serves 8

SPLIT OPEN THE VANILLA BEANS with a knife and scrape the seeds into a large bowl. Discard the pods. Add 7 egg yolks and beat vigorously with a whisk. Pour in the sugar and beat until the mixture whitens. Incorporate the milk and mix until the mixture is homogenous and smooth. Incorporate the cream and set the mixture aside to rest for at least 1 hour in the refrigerator. Foam will rise to the surface. Just skim it off with a spoon.

Preheat the oven to 200°F (95°C).

Fill in eight 4-inch (10-cm) ramekins with the egg mixture to only about ½ inch (1.5 cm) deep. Place the ramekins in a shallow dish with water coming halfway up the sides. Place the bain-marie in the oven and cook for 45 minutes. The custards must be firm but not hard—they will jiggle a bit when shaken. Allow custards to cool in the refrigerator.

Sprinkle the surface of the cold custards with sugar and caramelize with a torch or under the broiler (close to the element) until the top is golden brown. Return the ramekins to the refrigerator and serve cold.

SUGGESTED WINES
Banyuls Domaine de la Casa Blanca, France
or Pipe, Sumac Ridge, BC

This can be a surprising and spectacular dessert to serve to your guests. It's easy to make, and certainly less expensive than other desserts. In the summer months you can omit the crème anglaise and pour a fruit coulis in the bottom of a glass. Place the floating island on top, add a sprig of mint and serve with madeleines (see page 134).

Floating Islands
OEUFS À LA NEIGE

Islands

3 ½ cups (900 mL) milk

8 eggs

Pinch salt

⅓ cup (80 mL) sugar

Crème Anglaise

⅔ cup (160 mL) of the milk from the Islands ingredients

1 vanilla bean

¾ cup (180 mL) whipping cream

4 egg yolks

⅓ cup (80 mL) sugar

ISLANDS

IN A WIDE SAUCEPAN, heat the milk to just under a simmer.

Separate the eggs and beat the egg whites with a pinch of salt. Incorporate the sugar little by little, until stiff peaks form. With a tablespoon, drop a spoonful of egg white into simmering milk and cook for 2 minutes, turning over with a slotted spoon and cooking again for 2 minutes. Drain on a paper towel and repeat the procedure. If your pot is large enough you can cook 5 or 6 islands at a time. Keep in the refrigerator until needed.

CRÈME ANGLAISE

Transfer 2/3 cup (160 mL) of the cooking milk to a medium pot. Split the vanilla bean open, scrape out the seeds, and set aside; add the pod to the milk. Add the cream and bring to a simmer.

In a large bowl, whisk the egg yolks with the sugar and vanilla seeds for 3 to 4 minutes. Slowly incorporate the hot milk while stirring constantly. Pour the mixture back into the pot over medium heat and cook without bringing to a boil. Stir constantly with a wooden spoon. Remove from the heat, discard vanilla pods, and stir slowly until the custard is completely smooth and silky. The crème anglaise is ready when it leaves a trace on the back of a spoon when you run your finger through it. As soon as it is ready, immerse the pot in a bowl filled with ice to stop cooking.

CARAMEL

In a small pot, mix the sugar and water. Melt over medium heat, all the while moistening the sides of the pot with a wet brush so that the caramel does not crystallize. Remove the caramel from the heat when it is a deep golden colour.

To serve the islands, pour the crème anglaise into a large serving bowl, top with islands, and pour a thin stream of caramel on top.

SUGGESTED WINES

Champagne Pommery, France
or Brut Sparkling Wine, Blue Mountain, BC

Caramel

¾ cup (180 mL) sugar

4 Tbsp water

Preparation time: 20 minutes
Cooking time: 20 minutes
Serves 6 to 8

Summer

I HAVE VIVID MEMORIES of my childhood summers in France. At nighttime, the family dined outside on the terrace. My grandmother was the cook in the family. For the children, she often prepared an iced red wine soup for which she'd boil red wine with a great amount of sugar. When the alcohol evaporated, she'd drown the soup with ice cubes, pour it in a bowl, and serve it with thick slices of bread.

Every day, we swam in Le Loeng, a river in Fontainebleau. Around 4:30 in the afternoon, the ice cream trolley's bell rang, and it was a race to indulge in sweet treats.

Now I indulge in the voluptuous fruits of summer: the tender and fragrant flesh of the peach within its velvety robe; the flawless skin and lush liqueur of the cherry; the enchantment of a strawberry or raspberry still covered with morning dew—like biting into heaven.

The mixture of sea and earth (tuna and cheese) isn't a simple marriage, but it's very good and can be surprising. Serve this carpaccio with a glass of freshly made tomato juice stirred with an ounce of vodka. It's vachement bon!

Tuna Carpaccio with Sheep Cheese

CARPACCIO DE THON AUX LAMELLES DE FROMAGE DE BREBIS

2 lb (1 kg) ahi tuna fillet

¼ lb (125 g) sea salt

½ cup (125 mL) good-quality extra virgin olive oil (French, if possible)

Salt and pepper

⅓ cup (80 mL) lemon juice (about 3 lemons)

3 Tbsp (45 mL) finely chopped red shallots

2 Tbsp (30 mL) finely chopped chives

¾ lb (375 g) Tomme or other dry sheep cheese (specialty cheese shop)

Preparation time: 30 minutes
Rest time: 12 hours in the refrigerator
Serves 6

PLACE THE TUNA FILLET on a plate and cover with the sea salt. Cover the plate with plastic wrap and let rest for 12 hours in the refrigerator.

Rinse the fillet abundantly under cold running water and pat dry. Sprinkle with half of the olive oil and return to the refrigerator to keep cold.

With a long, sharp knife, cut the tuna fillet into the thinnest possible slices. On 6 plates, arrange the slices in one layer. Season lightly with salt and pepper. Sprinkle with the lemon juice, the remaining olive oil, shallots, and chives and keep in the refrigerator until serving. Just before serving, add sheep cheese slivers on top.

A side of garden salad with fresh herbs and a thick slice of toasted country bread go well with this dish.

SUGGESTED WINES
Riesling, Hugel, France
or Riesling, Wild Goose, BC

Omelet Cake

GÂTEAU D'OMELETTE

1 eggplant

1 zucchini

5 Tbsp (75 mL) olive oil

1 red pepper, diced

1 green pepper, diced

1 onion, diced

2 tomatoes

8 eggs

Salt and pepper

6 basil leaves, chopped

1 clove garlic, crushed

Extra virgin olive oil

2 Tbsp (30 mL) lemon juice

Preparation time: 20 minutes
Cooking time: 1 hour and 45 minutes
Resting time: 6 hours
Serves 6

On a warm, starry night on the patio, this is the ideal dish, as summer flavours meld on your plate. The recipe reminds me of one of Brigitte's favourites: a very cold ratatouille topped with a soft-boiled egg. Break the yolk and let it run through the ratatouille. Top with a dash of quality olive oil. Life is good!

WITHOUT PEELING, slice the eggplant and zucchini lengthwise into ⅛-inch (3-mm) slices. Heat 2 Tbsp (30 mL) of the olive oil in a large pan and lightly brown the slices over medium-high heat. Absorb the excess oil with paper towels. Line an 8½ x 4½-inch (1.5-L) loaf pan with the eggplant and the zucchini.

In the same pan, heat the remaining 3 Tbsp (45 mL) olive oil over medium-low heat and sweat the peppers and the onion until softened. Drain and set aside to cool.

Preheat the oven to 400°F (200°C).

Put the tomatoes in a bowl of boiling water for a few seconds. Slip off the peels, remove the seeds, drain, and chop. In a bowl, mix the eggs with salt and pepper; add the peppers, onions, tomatoes, basil, and garlic. Pour this mixture over the eggplant and zucchini and cover with aluminum foil. Place the loaf pan in a larger ovenproof dish; fill with water so that it comes halfway up the sides of the pan. Bake in the bain-marie for 1 hour and 45 minutes. When cooked, cool for 6 hours in the refrigerator.

Carefully unmould the omelet cake and slice into 6 portions. Before serving, drizzle with extra virgin olive oil and lemon juice.

SUGGESTED WINES
Hermitage Blanc, Guigal, France
or Viognier, Jackson Triggs, BC

The ideal place to serve this tart is on a secluded beach, perhaps protected by rocks on each side. And don't forget the white wine—keep it cool by placing it in the cold water. Bon appétit!

Clam and Parsley Tart
TARTE AUX COQUES ET PERSIL

Pastry

1 cup (250 mL) all-purpose flour

¾ cup (180 mL) softened unsalted butter

¼ cup (60 mL) water

Pinch salt

Filling

2 lb (1 kg) clams in shell

1 Tbsp (15 mL) sea salt

1 cup (250 mL) white wine

1 onion, peeled, washed, and diced

1 sprig thyme

2 bay leaves

4 whole black peppercorns

4 eggs

½ cup (125 mL) whipping cream

2 sprigs flat-leaf parsley, chopped

Preparation time: 45 minutes
Cooking time: 30 minutes
Resting time: 1 hour in refrigerator
Serves 6

PASTRY

PLACE FLOUR, BUTTER, WATER, AND SALT in the bowl of a stand mixer or a food processor with a plastic blade, kneading the dough until it's well mixed. When ready, roll into a ball, cover with plastic wrap, and refrigerate for 1 hour.

Roll the dough out on a floured surface and spread onto an 8-inch (20-cm) buttered pie dish.

FILLING

Preheat the oven to 400°F (200°C).

Rinse the clams several times with lots of water. Sprinkle the clams with salt and leave to drain 15 minutes (to release the sand). Rinse again.

In a large pot, combine the wine, onion, thyme, bay leaves, and whole peppercorns. Bring to a boil and add the clams. Steam 5 to 7 minutes until the clams open. Once open, remove them from their shells and distribute evenly in the prepared crust.

In a bowl, mix the eggs, cream, and parsley until smooth. Pour over the clams, season with salt and pepper, and bake for 30 minutes.

SUGGESTED WINES
Muscadet Louis Maitereau, France
or Semillon, La Frenz, BC

This savoury dish is best served in late summer when ripe tomatoes and fresh basil are at their peak. Enjoy it on your patio or deck and pair it with your favourite rosé.

Tomato and Basil Tart

TARTE À LA TOMATE ET AU BASILIC

Crust

¾ cup (180 mL) butter, cold

1 cup (250 mL) all-purpose flour

Pinch salt

1 Tbsp (15 mL) chopped fresh rosemary

1 cup (250 mL) ice water

Filling

6 ripe tomatoes

2 buffalo mozzarella balls
(fine Italian grocery stores)

2 Tbsp (30 mL) pitted, sliced black olives
(from Nice if possible!)

6 anchovies

3 leaves basil, torn

2 Tbsp (30 mL) pesto sauce
(see page 138)

Preparation time: 30 minutes
Cooking time: 40 minutes
Serves 6 to 8

CRUST

CUT THE COLD BUTTER INTO CUBES and put in the food processor with a plastic blade. Add the flour, salt, and rosemary. Mix until the texture is sandy. Add the water and stop the processor as soon as a ball forms. Wrap the dough in plastic wrap and refrigerate for 20 minutes.

Preheat the oven to 350°F (180°C).

Place the dough on a floured working surface. Working the dough from the centre out, use quick strokes with a rolling pin to a thickness of about ⅛ inch (3 mm). Set in a buttered 9-inch (23-cm) pie pan.

FILLING

Put the tomatoes in a bowl of boiling water for a few seconds. Slip off the skins, cut the tomatoes in quarters, remove the seeds, and drain. Cut the mozzarella into round slices.

In the prepared crust, layer the tomatoes and mozzarella on the bottom. Add the olives, anchovies, and basil on top. Coat with pesto sauce and bake in the preheated oven for 30 to 40 minutes. Serve from the pie dish.

SUGGESTED WINES

Tavel Rosé Château d'Aqueria, France
or Pinot Gris, Nichol Vineyard, BC

If I had to choose just one product from Italy, it would be Parmesan, the king of cheeses. When I cut a piece open, it's a sensual experience—the texture, the aroma, the robust taste.

Parmesan Shortbread

SABLÉ AU PARMESAN

1 cup (250 mL) grated Parmesan cheese

1 cup (250 mL) all-purpose flour

1 cup (250 mL) soft unsalted butter

6 tomatoes, about 2 inches (5 cm) in diameter

Salt and pepper

¼ cup (60 mL) olive oil

Preparation time: 1 hour
Cooking time: 15 minutes
Rest time: 30 minutes
Serves 6

PLACE THE PARMESAN, flour and butter in the bowl of a stand mixer or a food processor with a plastic blade and mix until a dough is formed. Roll the dough into a ball, cover with plastic wrap, and refrigerate for 30 minutes.

Put the tomatoes in a bowl of boiling water for a few seconds. Slip off the skins, remove the seeds, and cut the tomatoes into thin slices. Sprinkle with salt and pepper so they lose a little of their water content.

Preheat the oven to 450°F (230°C).

Remove the dough from the refrigerator and let it sit at room temperature until you can roll it out to ⅛ inch (3 mm) thick without breaking. Cut it into 6 circles of 4 inches (10 cm) each. Place on a parchment-lined baking sheet and lay the tomato slices attractively on the pastry, leaving a border of ⅛ inch (3 mm). Bake in the preheated oven for 10 minutes. Allow to cool to room temperature.

With a spatula, carefully transfer the shortbreads onto 6 plates. (They are very fragile.) Drizzle with olive oil and season with salt and pepper. Serve with a green salad and Tapenade Vinaigrette (see page 139).

SUGGESTED WINES
Palette Rosé, Château Simone, France
or Pinot Gris, Burrowing Owl, BC

This recipe looks very simple to make, but sometimes simple recipes are the most difficult. You need to cook it very quickly, serve it immediately, and eat it at once. You cook; you eat.

Prawns Sautéed with Fresh Thyme

GROSSES CREVETTES POÊLÉES AU THYM FRAIS

16 prawns (16 to 20 per lb) uncooked, peeled and deveined

3 Tbsp (45 mL) whipping cream

2 Tbsp (30 mL) chopped fresh thyme

¼ cup (60 mL) all-purpose flour

¼ cup (60 mL) canola oil

Preparation time: 15 minutes
Cooking time: 5 minutes
Serves 4

PLACE THE PRAWNS in a bowl, pour the cream over, and add the thyme. Soak for 10 minutes.

Take the prawns out individually and coat lightly with flour, tapping to remove the excess. Heat the oil in a pan and sauté the prawns, 4 at a time, for 30 seconds on each side. Serve immediately accompanied with a mesclun salad.

SUGGESTED WINES
Menetou Salon Henri Pelle, France
or Pinot Grigio, D'Asolo, BC

54

If you ask someone from Marseilles what are life's most important things, they will say the birth of Christ and bouillabaisse, in that order. This soup was born from the rocky inlets running along the French Mediterranean coastline from Toulon to Marseilles and all the way to Martigues! Marseilles is, in fact, the dish's native town. Since most of the fish used in the original recipe can't be found here, you can replace with West Coast seafood, but please understand ... it can't be called a traditional bouillabaisse any longer. This is absolutely best when shared with good friends and served outdoors, with a nice rosé from Provence and the sound of cicadas in the air.

$\mathcal{B}$ouillabaisse

BOUILLABAISSE

Stock

2 lb (1 kg) fish, including whole rockfish
(such as: girelles and parrot fish),
a few heads and tails of conger eel,
horny shelled green crabs, perches
or
2 lb (1 kg) heads, bones, and tails
of white-fleshed fish
(ask your fishmonger)

2 Tbsp (30 mL) olive oil

2 small leeks, white parts only, chopped,

2 medium onions, peeled and chopped

2 cloves garlic, peeled and chopped

5 medium tomatoes, washed,
seeded, and chopped

2 fennel stalks, sliced

½ bay leaf

1 sprig parsley

1 tsp (5 mL) dried orange peel
(dry the zest of an orange overnight and
chop finely)

16 cups (4 L) boiling water

Salt and pepper

SCALE, GUT, AND RINSE ALL FISH if your fishmonger hasn't already done so.

STOCK

In a large pot, heat the olive oil and combine fish heads and bones, vegetables, bay leaf, parsley, and orange peel. Sauté at low heat for 10 to 15 minutes until soft, but not coloured. Pour boiling water over the fish and vegetables. Bring to a soft boil and cook for 30 minutes. Strain the hot mixture through a fine sieve, pressing out juices with the back of a wooden spoon. Discard the solids and season the stock with salt and pepper. Set aside.

56

Bouillabaisse

Cut the potatoes into 1-inch (2.5-cm) slices. Put the fish and potatoes in a heavy-bottomed pot and cover with the reserved stock. Do not add the shellfish yet. Add the olive oil and saffron. If there is not enough stock to cover the fish, add a little water. Bring to a boil and simmer for 12 minutes over medium heat. Add the shellfish of your choice and cook 5 minutes longer.

To serve, remove the fish and shellfish with a slotted spoon and carefully transfer to shallow serving dishes. Ladle some hot stock over the fish, just to cover. Pass the navette slices and rouille separately, and eat as much as you like.

ROUILLE

In a mortar, pound the pimentos, garlic, and ¼ cup (60 mL) of the olive oil into a paste. Season with salt. Moisten the breadcrumbs with some stock and squeeze out the excess liquid. Add the moistened crumbs a spoonful at a time to the mortar, and pound until smooth. Add the remaining olive oil little by little, stirring with the pestle all the time. Continue until the sauce is thick and smooth. Add 1 tsp (5 mL) of stock if the sauce separates. The rouille must have the consistency of a sauce, not of a mayonnaise.

The rouille is essential for bouillabaisse, but you can also flavour and thicken sauces with it or add it to creamy salad dressings for seafood.

SUGGESTED WINES

Rosé de Provence Domaine d'Ott, France
or Pinot Blanc, Quails' Gate, BC

Bouillabaisse

3 big, long, narrow potatoes,
washed and peeled

4 lb (2 kg) whole fish or slices of
fish such as: scorpion fish (rascasse),
weevers (vives), monkfish (baudroie),
eel (anguille), gunard (galinette),
John Dory (Saint-Pierre),
Spanish lobsters (cigales)
or
Scallops, prawns, mussels, clams,
salmon, snapper, marlin, tuna,
mahi mahi, cod

2 tsp (10 mL) olive oil

2 saffron strands

Navette Bread (see page 142)

Rouille

2 small fresh red pimento peppers
or similar medium-hot chilies,
seeded and diced

2 cloves garlic, chopped

1 cup (250 mL) olive oil

Salt

Handful slightly dried bread crumbs

2–3 tsp (10–15 mL) stock from the soup

Preparation time: 1½ hours
Cooking time: 40 minutes
Serves 8

The traditional quiche Lorraine doesn't call for any cheese. So don't add too much cheese, or you'll mask the taste of the other ingredients. In this version, I use only a small quantity of Swiss cheese. Slices make a nice appetizer, or serve it for lunch with greens tossed in nut oil.

Ham and Cheese Quiche

QUICHE LORRAINE

Crust

3¼ cups (800 mL) flour

¾ cup + 2 Tbsp (205 mL) potato starch (also called potato flour)

½ lb (250 g) butter, at room temperature

1 tsp (5 mL) salt

7 egg yolks

⅓ cup + 2 Tbsp (100 mL) water

CRUST

PUT ALL THE CRUST INGREDIENTS in the food processor with a plastic mixing blade, and mix at a low speed until the dough does not adhere to the sides. Wrap the dough in plastic wrap and refrigerate for 1 hour.

Place the cold dough on a floured working surface. Roll the dough from the centre out, using quick strokes with a rolling pin, to a thickness of about ⅛ inch (3 mm). Place in a buttered 9-inch (23-cm) pie pan. Trim off the excess dough. Pierce holes in the bottom with a fork. Cover the dough with plastic wrap and let rest in the refrigerator for a minimum of 30 minutes. Refrigeration will prevent the dough from shrinking while baking.

Preheat the oven to 200°C (400°F).

Cover the cold piecrust with a piece of fitted parchment paper and fill up to the top with dry beans. Bake for 15 minutes or until lightly coloured. Remove the piecrust from the oven; remove beans and parchment paper. Let cool in the mould. Keep the oven at the same temperature.

FILLING

While the piecrust is baking, blanch the bacon pieces for a few minutes in boiling water to eliminate excess salt and fat; drain. Heat a medium pan over high heat and sauté bacon until crisp.

Place the crisp bacon on the dough and top with the minced ham. Spread the grated Swiss cheese over top and set aside.

In a medium bowl, whisk together the eggs, milk, cream, nutmeg, salt and pepper. Pour this mixture over the meat and cheese, all the way to the top of the dough. Bake for 40 minutes, until the cream is set and the top is a nice light brown.

SUGGESTED WINES

Merlot, Christian Moueix, France
or Merlot, Red Rooster, BC

Filling

4 oz (100 g) thick bacon, cut in ½-inch (1-cm) strips (about ⅔ cup/150 mL)

6–8 slices cooked ham, finely minced

2 Tbsp (30 mL) grated Swiss cheese

4 large eggs

⅔ cup (160 mL) milk

¾ cup + 2 Tbsp (200 mL) light cream

Nutmeg, salt and pepper

Preparation time: 1½ hours
Cooking time: 55 minutes
Serves 6

OOOOOHHH!!!
PLEASE TELL ME THAT'S THE SMELL
OF THE CHEESE AND NOT **FEET**!!!

Buy a rabbit between 3 and 5 lb (1.5 to 2.2 kg). This is a perfect size for the best-quality rabbit—larger ones are tough. The mustard sauce entirely coats and flavours each piece of rabbit. As we say in France, it's meu-meu, *an expression that means "really good." Chinon, a fruity Cabernet Franc from the Loire, makes it even better.*

Rabbit with Mustard Sauce

LAPIN À LA MOUTARDE

One 3–5-lb (1.5–2.2-kg) rabbit (fine meat markets)

1 small bunch tarragon

⅓ cup (80 mL) Dijon mustard

1 tsp (5 mL) olive oil

3 Tbsp (45 mL) lemon juice

2 bay leaves, cut in two

Salt and pepper

1 cup (250 mL) whipping cream

½ cup (125 mL) dry white wine

Preparation time: 30 minutes
Cooking time: 45 minutes
Serves 4

ASK YOUR BUTCHER to cut the rabbit in 5 pieces (2 front legs, 2 rear legs, and the saddle) and debone the saddle. Stuff the saddle with tarragon, reserving a few leaves as garnish, and tie it up like a roast. In a blender, emulsify the Dijon mustard (reserving 1 Tbsp/15 mL) with the olive oil, lemon juice, bay leaves, and salt and pepper. Brush the rabbit pieces generously with the mixture, setting aside what you don't use in a bowl.

Preheat the oven to 475°F (240°C).

In an ovenproof skillet, sear the rabbit and brown lightly. Transfer the skillet to the oven and cook for 30 minutes.

To the bowl with the reserved mustard mixture, add the cream, wine, and reserved Dijon mustard. Mix well. Remove the rabbit from the oven, skim off the excess fat, and deglaze with the creamy mustard mixture. Make sure to scrape up all drippings. Return the rabbit pieces and cook for 5 to 7 minutes more.

Divide the saddle in 4 and place the rabbit pieces in a serving dish. Finish with fresh whole tarragon leaves and serve with fresh tagliatelle or fettuccini noodles.

SUGGESTED WINES
Chinon Charles Joguet, France
or Cabernet Franc, Fairview Cellars, BC

The two best ways to enjoy fennel are braised very slowly in the oven with a few spices, or raw and marinated. This recipe brings a sunshine smile to my face; it's a perfectly intense and crisp summer dish.

Orange-Flavoured Fennel Salad and Prawns

SALADE DE FENOUIL À L'ORANGE ET CREVETTES

2 large fennel bulbs

Salt and pepper

2 Tbsp (30 mL) lemon juice
(or one large lemon)

¼ cup (60 mL) freshly squeezed
orange juice

½ cup (125 mL) virgin olive oil

12 prawns

3 Tbsp (45 mL) virgin olive oil

4–5 sprigs dill

Preparation time: 20 minutes
Marinating time: 1–2 hours
Serves 6

TWO HOURS BEFORE serving the salad, cut the fennel bulbs in half lengthwise and remove the core. Thinly slice the halves lengthwise. Place the slices in a large salad bowl and season with salt and pepper. Add the lemon juice, orange juice and the ½ cup (125 mL) oil. Stir well and let marinate in the refrigerator for at least one hour.

Just before serving the salad, sauté the prawns in the remaining 3 Tbsp (45 mL) oil on high heat. Place on the cold marinated salad. Garnish with dill.

SUGGESTED WINES
Bandol Blanc Domaine Pibarnon, France
or White Meritage, Red Rooster, BC

This recipe is full of the flavours of Moroccan cuisine. I love this cuisine for its colours and perfumes, and also because it's the real cuisine of the women of Morocco, for they're the ones who prepare all the food in that country.

Chicken with Lemon Confit

POULET AU CONFIT DE CITRON

Lemon Confit

6 organic lemons, washed

½ cup (125 mL) sugar

Stew

2 chickens, 3–4 lb (1.5–2 kg) each

12 tomatoes

¼ cup (60 mL) extra virgin olive oil

2 onions, peeled and minced

3 fennel bulbs, trimmed
and sliced lengthwise

2 Tbsp (30 mL) tomato paste

6 cloves garlic, crushed

3 Tbsp (45 mL) ground cumin

Salt and freshly ground pepper

One 12-oz (340-g) box couscous
(optional)

Preparation time: 40 minutes
Cooking time: 40 minutes
Serves 6

LEMON CONFIT

WITH THE PEEL ON, cut the lemons in quarters lengthwise. Place them in a small, heavy-bottomed pot with the sugar. Add water just to cover. Simmer for about 45 minutes, until you can see through the lemons. Set aside.

STEW

Have your butcher cut each chicken into 7 pieces. Submerge the tomatoes for a few seconds in a pot of boiling water. Slip off the skins, remove the seeds, drain, and dice.

Heat half the olive oil in a pan at medium-high heat and sear and brown the chicken on all sides.

In a large sauté pan, heat the remaining oil and sweat the onions and fennel for a few minutes. Stir in the tomato paste and garlic, then add the chicken to the pan. Remove the lemons from the syrup and add to the chicken. Add the diced tomatoes and half of the thickened lemon juice. Season with cumin, salt, and pepper. Cover and simmer for about 35 minutes. Serve with couscous, prepared according to package directions.

SUGGESTED WINES
Saint Nicolas de Bourgueil, Vincent Grégoire, France
or Cabernet Franc, Burrowing Owl, BC

Potato Blinis

BLINIS AUX POMMES DE TERRE

5 medium potatoes

3 Tbsp (45 mL) all-purpose flour

3 eggs

4 egg whites

3 Tbsp (45 mL) whipping cream

¼ cup (60 mL) milk

¼ cup (60 mL) clarified butter
(see page 138)

Salt and pepper

Preparation time: 15 minutes
Cooking time: 35 minutes
Serves 6 to 8

These blinis can be served with so many things: the Creamy Chicken Fricassée (see page 30), smoked salmon, or caviar. You can even sprinkle them with icing sugar and serve them for dessert. If you want a different taste, add chopped chives, sliced almonds or chopped olives, etc.

PEEL THE POTATOES and simmer them in salted water until soft. Drain and mash. Let the potatoes cool off.

With a whisk, mix the cold mashed potatoes with the flour, adding the whole eggs one at the time. Add the egg whites (not beaten), the cream, and the milk and mix well.

Pour 1 Tbsp (15 mL) of clarified butter at a time into a hot frying pan. For each portion, drop a soupspoon of batter in the hot butter. When one side is lightly coloured, flip the blini over and cook the other side.

SUGGESTED WINES
Champagne, Moët et Chandon, France
or Sparkling Brut, Blue Mountain, BC

Le Pot de Rillettes

Le Pot d'oeufs de Saumon
9.80

La Planche de Saumon
9.75 Fumé
Assiette De 6 Huîtres 70

La Planche de Saucisson sec
8.50
Assiette de Fromages
8

POTATO BLINIS
PAGE 64

ORANGE-FLAVOURED FENNEL SALAD AND PRAWNS
PAGE 62

HAM AND CHEESE QUICHE
PAGE 58

APRICOT TART
PAGE 65

Apricot Tart

TARTE AUX ABRICOTS

1 sheet frozen puff pastry
(thaw according to package directions)

20 small, round ripe apricots

¾ cup (180 mL) sugar

½ cup (125 mL) unsalted butter,
cut in small cubes

Powdered sugar

Good-quality vanilla ice cream

Preparation time: 20 minutes
Cooking time: 30 minutes
Serves 4

In France, apricots have a poetic nickname, "oeufs du soleil," loosely translated as "sun's eggs." The recipe is very easy, but the quality of the fruit will make all the difference. Buy ripe fruit and make sure it isn't too soft or mealy. If apricots are picked unripe, they'll never ripen. Look for them in July.

SPREAD THE PUFF PASTRY into a rectangle 8 x 4 inches (20 x 10 cm). Prick the dough with a fork. Transfer onto parchment paper spread on a baking sheet. Put in the refrigerator for 10 minutes.

Preheat the oven to 325°F (160°C).

Cut the apricots in half and remove the stones, skin side on your working surface. Remove the puff pastry from the refrigerator and place the apricots tightly, skin side up, on the pastry. Sprinkle with the sugar and sprinkle the small pieces of butter evenly over top. Place in the oven and bake for about 30 minutes. Place on a serving dish immediately, dust with powdered sugar, and serve warm with a scoop of vanilla ice cream.

SUGGESTED WINES
Gewürztraminer, Vendange Tardive, Colette Faller, France
or Late Harvest Riesling, Hillside, BC

Nougat Parfait

NOUGAT GLACÉ

3 Tbsp (45 mL) candied orange skins

¼ cup (60 mL) dried currants

¼ cup (60 mL) Grand Marnier

½ cup (125 mL) sugar

½ cup (125 mL) sliced almonds

¼ cup (60 mL) shelled chopped pistachios

1 cup (250 mL) sugar

¼ cup (60 mL) water

6 egg whites

½ cup (125 mL) liquid honey

3 cups (750 mL) whipping cream

2 cups (500 mL) red-berry coulis (see page 141)

Preparation time: 1 hour
Resting time: 5 to 6 hours
Serves 6 to 10

This uses a mixture of dried fruit, nuts, and candied fruit. These are all part of the twelve traditional small desserts served in Provence over the Christmas holiday. A slice of this dessert is customarily served with a spoonful of red-berry coulis (see page 141).

CHOP THE CANDIED orange skins and soak with the currants for 15 minutes in the Grand Marnier.

Preheat the oven to 250°F (120°C).

In an ovenproof pan, mix the ½ cup (125 mL) sugar with the almonds and pistachios. Heat in the oven until they caramelize. Let the mixture harden, then transfer to a board and break it into pieces with a large knife.

In a small pot, mix the 1 cup (250 mL) sugar and the water to make the syrup. Cook until you reach 230° to 250° F (105° to 120°C) on a candy thermometer, or until the syrup forms small, hard balls when dropped into a glass of cold water.

In a large bowl, beat the egg whites at medium-high speed with a mixer. Keep the beaters going while adding the next ingredients. When the syrup has reached 250°F (120°C), pour slowly into the egg whites and beat until mixture is completely cooled. Add the honey and mix some more.

In another bowl, beat the whipping cream until soft peaks form. With a large rubber spatula, gently fold the cream into the meringue. Add the candied fruit, caramelized nuts, and soaking liquid and fold until well mixed.

Line an 8 x 4-inch (1.5-L) loaf pan with plastic wrap. Pour in the nougat and freeze for 5 to 6 hours.

Run warm water on the outside of the loaf pan to transfer nougat onto a cutting board. Cut in slices and serve with a splash of red-berry coulis on top.

SUGGESTED WINES
Gewürztraminer Grains Nobles, Hugel, France
or Riesling Ice Wine, Mission Hills, BC

You need fresh cherries for this dessert. Sour ones—Morello or Montmorency—give a good balance between the sweet dough and the fruit. The sourness excites the palate. Don't pit the cherries; it helps keep the juice inside the skin. The anticipation of an explosion of taste with each cherry will delight you.

Warm Cherry Clafoutis
CLAFOUTIS AUX CERISES

1 lb (500 g) fresh cherries
(not too sweet!)

2 tsp (10 mL) butter, plus more to
butter the dish

All-purpose flour for dusting

1¼ cups (300 mL) milk

1 vanilla bean, split lengthwise,
seeds removed

3 eggs

Pinch salt

1 cup (250 mL) sugar

½ cup (125 mL) all-purpose flour

Preparation time: 30 minutes
Cooking time: 30 minutes
Serves 4

WASH THE CHERRIES and pit if you wish (I prefer to leave the pits in.) Butter and flour a 10-inch (25-cm) ceramic flan dish.

Preheat the oven to 350°F (180°C).

In a small pot, bring the milk, vanilla bean and vanilla seeds to a boil over medium heat. Add the 2 tsp (10 mL) butter to the milk.

In a bowl, beat together the eggs, a pinch of salt, and the sugar. With a hand-held beater, mix until the mixture whitens. Incorporate the flour, mixing constantly. Remove the vanilla bean from the milk and slowly pour the warm milk into the egg mixture, beating vigorously all the while. Pour the mixture into the dish and add the cherries evenly throughout the dish. Bake for 20 to 30 minutes, until golden brown on top.

Serve at room temperature accompanied with a red-berry coulis (see page 141).

SUGGESTED WINES
Bourgueil Thierry Boucard, France
or Pinot Noir, Quails' Gate, BC

Autumn

FALL IN FRANCE is the season to harvest not only vegetables, but grapes. There's a tradition of purchasing parts of the grape harvest, or *achat en primeur*. The grower keeps your portion of the wine until it's bottled, one to two years later. This practice is common in France. A great treat I remember is called *bourru*: pure, freshly squeezed grape juice, not yet fermented, sold in bottles.

Fall meant game season, the perfect time of the year to serve an impeccably roasted partridge accompanied by crisp toasts with cooked liver spread. In my restaurant or at home, I'd prepare dishes like Lièvre (hare) à la Royale, Fricassée de Garenne, biches (deer), and sarcelles (teal duck).

Fall is also the last layer of fruit in what translates as "bachelor's jam." In the spring, a mix of the first fruits of the season is put in a jar and covered with sugar and grappa. Then summer fruits are added, and in the fall it's finished off with plums. This tasty jam is traditionally served at Christmastime with warm brioches.

Oyster Soup

SOUPE AUX HUÎTRES

Use medium-sized oysters. You want plump, meaty oysters that will explode with a fresh, pungent taste of the sea when you bite into them. Too large and the flavour will be diffused, too small and the taste isn't strong enough.

16 shucked oysters (reserve their juice)

5 red shallots, finely chopped

2 cups (500 mL) white wine

¼ cup (60 mL) whipping cream

2 Tbsp (30 mL) unsalted butter

Handful baby spinach leaves

Pepper

Preparation time: 25 minutes
Cooking time: 15 minutes
Serves 4

STRAIN THE OYSTERS in a sieve reserving the juices. Place 4 oysters in each serving bowl.

In a medium saucepan, put shallots, white wine, cream and butter. Bring to a boil and simmer for 15 minutes. Add the reserved juices and the spinach and cook for 30 more seconds.

Pour the soup over the oysters to warm them up. Add freshly cracked pepper just before serving.

SUGGESTED WINES
Graves Blanc, Château Fieuzal, France
or Reserve Chardonnay, Blue Mountain, BC

Pumpkin Soup
POTAGE DE POTIRONS

1 lb (500 g) pumpkin or squash flesh

3 cups water

Salt

1 cup (250 mL) whipping cream

Pinch ground nutmeg

1 egg yolk

1 bunch parsley, chopped

1 cup (250 mL) grated Swiss Emmenthal cheese

Preparation time: 20 minutes
Cooking time: 35 minutes
Serves 6

You'll find many different kinds of pumpkins and squashes at the market, with flesh ranging from pale yellow to deep orange. They all belong to the same family, and you can use any type you want for this soup. This is a great dish to serve at Thanksgiving.

CUT THE PUMPKIN in large pieces. Peel, seed, and remove the fibers. Cut in 1-inch (2.5-cm) cubes and place in a large pot. Cover with the water, add salt, and bring to a boil. Simmer for 30 minutes. Strain and reserve the water.

Purée the pumpkin in a food processor and transfer into a heavy-bottomed medium pot. Add 2 cups (500 mL) of the reserved water and ¾ cup (180 mL) of the cream. Bring to a boil, add nutmeg, and check the seasoning.

In a bowl, whisk the remaining cream with the yolk and chopped parsley. Stir the mixture into the soup and remove the soup from the heat. Serve very hot and pass the Swiss cheese separately for sprinkling on top.

SUGGESTED WINES
Macon Blanc, Jean Thevenet, France
or Pinot Blanc, Burrowing Owl, BC

In my native country, this is nicknamed des couilles d'ânes *("donkey's balls") because of the purple colour of the eggs. But when you break the poached eggs, the yellow yolks and the red wine make an unctuous sauce for dipping toast.*

Poached Eggs in Red Wine
OEUFS POCHÉS MEURETTE

8 slices back bacon

3 Tbsp (45 mL) cold unsalted butter

½ cup (125 mL) finely chopped onion (or shallots for a more subtle flavour)

2 cups (500 mL) red wine (preferably from Burgundy)

1 cup (250 mL) concentrated veal stock (specialty grocery stores)

Salt and pepper

8 thin slices country bread

2 cloves garlic, halved

¼ cup (60 mL) red wine vinegar

8 eggs

Preparation time: 30 minutes
Cooking time: 20 minutes
Serves 4

BLANCH THE BACK BACON in boiling water for 2 minutes. Remove and cut into wide, oblong chunks.

Heat 2 tsp (10 mL) of the butter in a pan and sauté the bacon and onion for 7 to 8 minutes at low heat, without browning. Pour in the wine and reduce to two-thirds. Add the veal stock and reduce to half. Pour the sauce into a narrow pot and season with salt and pepper. Keep warm. Just before serving, take the sauce off the heat and whisk in the remaining butter.

Grill the slices of bread, rub with the garlic, and place 2 slices in each soup plate.

To poach the eggs, simmer enough water in a wide pan to cover the eggs. Add the vinegar. Do not salt the water, as it will prevent the egg whites from coagulating properly. Break an egg into a cup and tilt as close to the surface as possible. Slide the egg into the liquid with a quick move of the wrist. Poach for 3 minutes, remove with a slotted spoon, and set on the sliced bread. You may cut off hanging white filaments from the egg. To serve, coat the eggs with the sauce.

SUGGESTED WINES
Volnay Domaine Marquis d'Angerville, France
or Pinot Noir, Nichol Vineyard, BC

Autumn is mushroom season. Whether you hunt them yourself or buy them in the markets, they're everywhere. You can easily preserve wild mushrooms and store the jars in a dark place until Christmas, when you can bring them out and serve them with crostini and good champagne.

Wild Mushrooms Marinated in Oil

CHAMPIGNONS DES BOIS MARINÉS À L'HUILE

2 lb (1 kg) wild mushrooms (chanterelles, cèpes/porcini, lobster mushrooms, etc.)

2 cups (500 mL) sunflower oil

Many bay leaves

1 tsp (5 mL) coarse, unrefined salt

1 tsp black peppercorns

Preparation time: 35 minutes
Cooking time: 2 hours
Yields one 4-cup (1-L) glass jar

SCRUB OR PEEL THE MUSHROOMS clean (do not wash under water). Separate the caps from the stalks and discard the stalks. Cut all into large slices. The smaller caps may be left whole. Heat ⅓ cup (80 mL) of the oil in a pan and sauté the mushrooms for 10 minutes at medium heat. Season with salt and pepper.

Place rows of mushrooms in a 4-cup (1-L) jar alternating with bay leaves, unrefined salt, and peppercorns. Cover with the remaining oil. Close the jar and immerse in a pot of water, sterilizing at a simmer for 2 hours from the time the water begins to boil.

These mushrooms can be enjoyed in an omelet or on crostini.

SUGGESTED WINES

Meursault Jean-François, Côte Dry, France
or Chardonnay, Township 7, BC

74

This dish is a bestseller at La Régalade. We use Bleu de Bresse, but if you can't find it, you can use Roquefort. I enjoy a piece of this tart with a glass of late-bottled port from my friend José's vineyard in Portugal.

Blue Cheese and Pear Tart

TARTE AUX POIRES ET FROMAGE BLEU

Tart

1 sheet frozen puff pastry
(thaw according to package instructions)

2 ripe pears

2 lemons, 1 halved, 1 thickly sliced

8 cups (2 L) water

2 cups (500 mL) sugar

4 thick slices Bleu de Bresse cheese

2 Tbsp (30 mL) unsalted butter

Salad

2 Tbsp (30 mL) red wine vinegar

Salt

¼ cup (60 mL) olive oil

2 Tbsp (30 mL) walnut oil

Pepper

⅓ lb (170 g) mixed greens

Preparation time: 20 minutes
Cooking time: 40 minutes
Serves 4

TART

CUT FOUR 5-INCH (12-cm) circles from your puff pastry sheet and place them on a baking sheet. Set aside.

Peel the pears and rub them with half a lemon. In a heavy, medium-sized saucepan, combine the water, sugar, and 3 or 4 lemon slices. Bring the syrup to a boil and cook for 5 minutes. Carefully drop in the pears. Simmer to poach for about 20 minutes (depending on the size of the pears). When poached, remove gently with a slotted spoon into a bowl to cool.

Preheat the oven to 325°F (160°C).

Top the puff pastry circles with a slice of cheese. Slice the cooled pears in half lengthwise and remove the core. Place a half pear over the cheese, cut-side down, and add dabs of butter. Bake in the preheated oven for about 10 minutes until the pastry is golden and the cheese bubbles.

SALAD

In a bowl, combine the wine vinegar and salt. Whisk while slowly adding the olive oil and walnut oil. Add pepper to taste. Just before serving, add the dressing to the mixed greens and serve beside the warm tart.

SUGGESTED WINES
Sainte Croix du Mont, Château Bélair, France
or Kerner Late Harvest, Gray Monk, BC

This is a wonderful condiment that complements a rustic terrine. It's delicious with cold sliced meat or cold cuts. I've included this recipe especially for Robert, my publisher!

Red Onion Compote

½ cup (125 mL) unsalted butter

¼ cup (60 mL) canola oil

2 large red onions, minced

2 cups (500 mL) red wine

½ cup (125 mL) sugar

Salt and pepper

Preparation time: 20 minutes
Cooking time: 50 minutes
Serves 6 to 8

IN A HEAVY-BOTTOMED POT, heat the butter and oil. Add the minced onions and cook over medium heat for 20 to 30 minutes, until tender. Add the red wine, sugar, salt, and pepper to taste and cook until the wine completely evaporates and the onions have a syrupy consistency. Transfer into an airtight container and cool in the refrigerator. This compote can keep for up to 3 weeks.

SUGGESTED WINES
Beaujolais Pisse Dru, France
or Gamay Noir, Blue Mountain, BC

Pineau des Charentes is an aperitif wine. This sweet concoction is the result of the addition of cognac to freshly pressed grape juice in order to prevent fermentation. The wine must stay in the cask one year and be bottled no sooner than October 1 of the next year (most respected houses keep it in the cask for an average of 5 years). You'll enjoy the subtle taste of the Pineau with this veal shank dish.

Braised Veal Shank in Pineau des Charentes

JARRET DE VEAU BRAISÉ AU PINEAU DES CHARENTES

2½ lb (1.2 kg) veal shank
cut 2 inches (5 cm) thick

Salt and pepper

¼ cup (60 mL) all-purpose flour

3 Tbsp (45 mL) unsalted butter

2 large leeks, white and tender green
parts only, cleaned and finely chopped

2 carrots, peeled and
cut into round slices

1 Tbsp (15 mL) sunflower oil

1 cup (250 mL) Pineau des Charentes
(liquor stores)

3 medium tomatoes, peeled,
seeded and chopped

2 cloves garlic, peeled and left whole

1 bouquet garni (see page 138)

Preparation time: 30 minutes
Cooking time: 2 hours
Serves 4

SEASON THE MEAT with salt and pepper and dredge in flour.

In a large, heavy-bottomed pot, heat half the butter; wilt the leeks and soften the carrots without browning. Using a slotted spoon, remove the vegetables and set aside.

Heat the remaining butter and the oil, searing the shank on all sides until golden brown. Season with salt and pepper and add the Pineau. Add the cooked carrots and leeks, tomatoes, garlic, and bouquet garni. Mix well and check the seasoning. Cover and simmer on low heat for 1½ hours. Turn the shanks over halfway through cooking time.

Serve in a ceramic serving dish accompanied by a macaroni bake (see page 140).

SUGGESTED WINES
Chinon Domaine Charles Joguet, France
or Gamay, Domaine de Chaberton, BC

I love the dense texture of halibut. You need to pay attention when you're cooking this; if you overcook halibut, the flaky quality disappears and the fish becomes cottony and flavourless. Cooking it with the skin on helps keep its moisture.

Saffron and Chorizo Halibut Boulangère
FLÉTAN BOULANGÈRE AU SAFRAN ET CHORIZO

2 lb (1 kg) chicken bones

1 carrot, cut in two

1 onion, quartered

4 whole cloves

13–15 chorizo sausage slices

1 bouquet garni (see page 138)

Salt and pepper

2 Tbsp (30 mL) vegetable oil

2 onions, sliced as thinly as possible

4 Yukon Gold potatoes, peeled, washed and cut into ¼-inch (5-mm) slices

12 saffron strands

Four ½-lb (250-g) halibut fillets, with skin

2 Tbsp (30 mL) grated Parmesan cheese

Preparation time: 30 minutes
Cooking time: 25 minutes
Serves 4

PLACE THE BONES in a large pot, add water to cover, plus the carrot, onion quarters pricked with the whole cloves, chorizo slices, and bouquet garni. Season with salt and pepper. Bring the stock to a boil and simmer for 20 to 25 minutes, skimming the surface regularly. Remove the stock from the heat, set the sausages aside, and discard the vegetables.

In a medium pot, heat the oil over low heat and sweat the sliced onions for 15 minutes, without letting them colour. Stir often to prevent the onions from sticking. Season with salt and pepper. Increase the heat to medium. Add the potato slices to the onions, cover with the chicken stock, and simmer for 15 minutes. Increase the heat to high. Bring the stock to a boil, add the saffron strands and cook for 5 to 6 minutes. Remove from the heat.

Preheat the oven to 425°F (220°C).

In a 12-inch (30-cm/3.5-L) ovenproof ceramic dish, place a row of sliced potatoes, then the chorizo slices. Place the halibut pieces on top and top with the remaining potatoes. Add enough cooking liquid just to cover the fish and potatoes. Sprinkle with Parmesan cheese, season with salt and pepper and bake for 10 to 15 minutes. Serve from the baking dish.

SUGGESTED WINES
Meursault, Domaine Leroy, France
or Pinot Gris, Burrowing Owl, BC

If you want to succeed in making a good confit, you need a large duck like a mallard, which is also used for foie gras. Don't think of this recipe as being fatty—the duck fat is rendered out during cooking, so the meat is crispy when done. When the potatoes are cooked in some of the duck fat, they take on the flavour of the duck. Delicious!

Duck Confit with Sarladaise Potatoes

CUISSES DE CANARD CONFITES, POMMES SARLADAISES

Confit

12 duck legs (fine meat shops)

3 cloves garlic

2 cups (500 mL) sea salt

3 sprigs thyme

4 bay leaves

1 small fresh red pimento, cut in half and seeded *or* 1 Tbsp/15 mL chopped red bell pepper

2 lb (1 kg) duck fat (fine meat shops)

CONFIT

PLACE THE DUCK LEGS in a large bowl. Cut one of the garlic cloves in half and rub the cut sides over the duck legs. Cover with salt, one sprig of thyme, and 2 bay leaves. Seal the dish with plastic wrap and leave in the refrigerator overnight.

The next day, preheat the oven to 300°F (150°C). Rinse the legs under cold water and pat dry. Place the legs in an oven dish that will hold them all in one layer. Sprinkle with 2 crushed cloves of garlic, 2 sprigs of thyme, 2 bay leaves, and the pimento. Cover the entire dish with the duck fat, keeping 2 heaping tablespoons aside. Place in the oven and roast for 2 hours. Do not allow it to boil. When done, let the duck legs rest in the fat at room temperature and prepare the potatoes. The recipe can be prepared up to this point and continued days, or even weeks, later because the fat preserves the meat.

POTATOES

Preheat the oven to 400°F (200°C).

Peel and wash the potatoes and slice into thick rounds. In a frying pan, heat the reserved duck fat over medium-high heat and sauté the potato slices until golden brown. Season the potatoes with salt and pepper, and add the clove of crushed garlic and the sliced truffle (if you have it). Sauté 1 more minute, then remove from the heat, but keep warm.

Place the duck legs in a shallow dish and cook in the pre-heated oven for 10 minutes to warm them up before adding to the potatoes.

Sprinkle the duck legs and sarladaise potatoes with parsley and serve with a chicory or curly endive salad.

SUGGESTED WINES

Côtes de Bergerac, Domaine du Bois de Pourquie, France
or Benchmark Cabernet Franc, Poplar Grove, BC

Potatoes

5 medium-sized potatoes

2 heaping Tbsp (25+ mL) duck fat

Salt and pepper

1 clove garlic, crushed

1 fresh truffle, finely sliced (optional)

1 Tbsp (15 mL) chopped parsley

One day ahead: prepare the
duck legs in salt
Preparation time: 40 minutes
Cooking time: 2 hours, 10 minutes
Serves 6

Wrap the endives with thin slices of gourmet deli ham (not packaged ham from the supermarket). The best endives are the short, rounded, compact ones—just like me! Here's a tip (or a truc *in French): add Roquefort to the béchamel for a different taste.*

Ham and Belgian Endives
ENDIVES AU JAMBON

Endives

8 Belgian endives

Unsalted butter for pans

Salt and pepper

1 lemon, washed and sliced

Water

8 slices cooked ham

Béchamel Sauce

¼ cup (60 mL) unsalted butter

¾ cup (180 mL) all-purpose flour

4 cups (1 L) milk

1 cup (250 mL) whipping cream

2 egg yolks

Preparation time: 40 minutes
Cooking time: 20 minutes
Serves 4

ENDIVES

PREHEAT THE OVEN to 325°F (160°C).

Wipe the endives clean and remove the core ends with a paring knife. Place the endives tightly in a buttered dish and season with salt and pepper. Lay the lemon slices on top and add enough water to cover. Cover with parchment paper and a plate, to keep the endives under water. Cook in the oven until the water is evaporated (around 30 minutes).

Wrap each endive with a slice of ham and place them side by side in another buttered ceramic baking dish. Set aside.

BÉCHAMEL SAUCE

Melt the butter without browning. When the butter is foaming, add the flour and cook at low heat for a few minutes, stirring constantly. When the flour is cooked, pour in the milk and all but a spoonful of the cream at once, and whisk until the sauce is smooth and no dry particles are left. Simmer for about 15 minutes and remove from the heat.

Preheat the broiler. In a small bowl, whisk together the 2 yolks and the extra spoonful of cream. Whisk the egg mixture into the sauce. Pour the sauce over the wrapped endives and broil until golden brown.

SUGGESTED WINES
Pouilly Fumé Les Silex, Didier Dagueneau, France
or Pinot Blanc, Mission Hill, BC

Coq au Vin

COQ AU VIN

One thing is certain; you should use a large, well-aged roasting hen for this dish, not a small and tender chicken. The very long cooking time wouldn't work with a tender bird. You'll want to dip your bread into the tasty sauce, and I say, go ahead.

Marinade

One 6–8-lb (2.7–3.5-kg) roasting chicken, cut into 16 pieces (ask your butcher to cut the chicken and to pack the ribs,

backbone and giblets separately for you)

3 large carrots, minced

1 large onion, minced

2 cloves garlic, crushed

¼ cup (60 mL) minced shallots

4 cups (1 L) red wine

2 Tbsp (30 mL) cognac

1 bouquet garni (see page 138)

6 whole black peppercorns

Stock

3 Tbsp (45 mL) grape seed oil

½ cup (125 mL) vegetable oil

¼ cup (60 mL) unsalted butter

1 chicken carcass and giblets

6 cups (1.5 L) chicken stock

MARINADE

PLACE THE CHICKEN pieces in a large bowl surrounded by two thirds of the carrots, two thirds of the onion, and all the garlic and shallots. Add the wine, cognac, bouquet garni, and peppercorns. Cover the bowl with plastic wrap and refrigerate for 24 hours.

STOCK

In a heavy-bottomed pot, heat the oils and butter. Sear the chicken bones and giblets with the remaining carrot and onion. Allow the mixture to sear for 5 to 10 minutes. Remove the fat, deglaze with the chicken stock, and bring to a boil. Simmer for 2 hours, regularly removing fat and foam from the surface. Remove the bones and strain the stock and vegetables through a sieve. Discard all solids, let the stock cool at room temperature, then refrigerate overnight.

TO FINISH

The following day, preheat the oven to 350°F (180°C).

Remove the chicken pieces from the marinade with a slotted spoon and pat dry. Set aside. Strain the marinade through a fine sieve into a medium-sized saucepan and set the aromatic vegetables aside. Bring the strained marinade to a boil, skimming the surface. Keep hot.

In a small saucepan, heat the chicken stock from the day before.

In a Dutch oven, heat the oil and butter over medium-high heat and sear the chicken pieces to a golden brown on all sides, starting on the skin side. When done, remove the chicken and set aside. Reduce the heat and add the aromatic vegetables from the marinade. Sweat them for 5 minutes, stirring to loosen any parts of chicken from the bottom of the pot. Place the pieces of chicken on top of the vegetables, splash the meat with the cognac and flambé. (A barbecue lighter is handy for this.) Add the hot marinade and simmer, allowing the liquid to reduce for about 10 minutes. Add the bouquet garni and enough warm chicken stock just to cover the meat. Cover and cook in the preheated oven for about 1½ hours. Check once in a while to make sure the dish is cooking evenly.

Meanwhile, blanch the bacon lardons in boiling water for 30 seconds. Pat dry and fry at medium-high heat (not to a crisp) in a frying pan. Drain on a paper towel and set aside. Keep a spoonful of the bacon fat in the pan. Sauté mushrooms (cut in quarters if the caps are large) in the bacon fat. Set aside. In the same pan, combine the pearl onions, a pinch of sugar and salt, and the butter. Add water to barely cover the onions. Cover loosely with parchment paper, bring to a boil, and simmer until the liquid has evaporated. Set aside in a separate bowl.

When the chicken is cooked, remove from the oven, skim the fat from the surface, and transfer the pieces to a large pot. Using a sieve, strain the sauce over the chicken and discard the vegetables. Season with salt and pepper. Add the bacon, pearl onions, and mushrooms and simmer over medium heat for 10 minutes.

CROUTONS

While the chicken simmers, make the croutons by heating some butter and walnut oil in a skillet and toasting the bread slices on each side. Remove from skillet and set aside on paper towels.

TO SERVE

Before serving, stir in the red wine vinegar and arrange the chicken in a serving dish. Pour the sauce over the chicken, surround the dish with the croutons, and sprinkle with chopped flat-leaf parsley. This dish can be served with buttered flat noodles.

SUGGESTED WINES
Savigny-les-Beaune, Domaine Doudet Naudin, France
or Pinot Noir Optimum, Gehringer, BC

To Finish

¼ cup (60 mL) grape seed oil

¼ cup (60 mL) unsalted butter

1 Tbsp (15 mL) cognac

1 bouquet garni

½ lb (250 g) slab bacon,
cut into lardons, strips ½ inch (1 cm)
thick and ¾ inch (2 cm) long

½ lb (250 g) white mushrooms,
cleaned and de-stemmed

40 pearl onions, peeled

Pinch sugar and salt

2 Tbsp (30 mL) unsalted butter

Croutons

Butter

Walnut oil

4 slices bread, cut into triangles

To Serve

4 tsp (20 mL) red wine vinegar

Chopped flat-leaf parsley

The day before:
prepare the marinade and stock
Preparation time: 1½ to 2 hours
Cooking time: 1½ to 2 hours
Serves 8

This most beautiful recipe brings together all the flavours of autumn: white mushrooms, chestnuts, and a very good Burgundy. "On peut refaire le monde autour de ce plat": *"We can recreate the world around this dish" when we share it with good friends by the fire.*

Duck Ragoût with Wild Mushrooms and Chestnuts

DAUBE DE CANARD AUX CÈPES ET CHÂTAIGNES

Duck and Marinade

8 cups (2 L) red wine

¼ cup (60 mL) Armagnac

2 large onions

2 carrots

5 oz (150 g) shelled chestnuts (vacuum packed, fine grocery store)

2 cloves garlic, crushed

1 bouquet garni (see page 138)

4 whole cloves

1 tsp whole black peppercorns

Salt

1 duck, boned and cut into 6 pieces (ask your butcher)

DUCK AND MARINADE

IN A LARGE BOWL mix the red wine and Armagnac in a large bowl. Peel, wash, and chop onions and carrots. Add vegetables, chestnuts, garlic, bouquet garni, cloves, peppercorns, and salt to the marinade. Place the duck pieces in the bowl, cover with plastic wrap and refrigerate overnight.

Ragoût

The following day, remove the duck pieces from the marinade with a slotted spoon, pat dry and set the duck and marinade aside.

In a large heavy-bottomed pot, heat 2 Tbsp (30 mL) of the duck fat and fry the duck pieces on both sides. Pour in the marinade and simmer, covered, at low heat for 3 hours.

In a frying pan, heat the remaining 1 Tbsp (15 mL) duck fat and sauté the mushrooms. Season with salt and pepper.

Ten minutes before the duck is cooked, add the mushrooms to the pot. Using a slotted spoon, transfer the duck and mushrooms to a big, shallow platter. In a small bowl, mix the butter and flour. Return the sauce to low heat and thicken with the butter mixture, dropping a bit at the time into the sauce and whisking constantly to avoid lumps. When the sauce is smooth, pour over the duck. Serve hot from the platter at the table.

Suggested wines
Mercurey Château de Chamirey, France
or Pinot Noir, Nichol Vineyard, BC

Ragoût

3 Tbsp (45 mL) duck fat
(fine meat shop)

1 lb (500 g) wild mushrooms
(cut in halves if too large)

Salt and pepper

1 Tbsp (15 mL) unsalted butter

1 Tbsp (15 mL) all-purpose flour

Salt and freshly ground pepper

The day before: prepare the marinade
Preparation time: 35 minutes
Cooking time: 3 hours
Serves 6

Potato Gratin

GRATIN DAUPHINOIS

6 large potatoes

2 cloves garlic, halved

¼ cup (60 mL) unsalted butter,
cut in small cubes

Salt and pepper

Nutmeg

Whipping cream
(the amount depends on
the size of the dish you use,
as the cream must cover
the potatoes entirely)

Preparation time: 15 minutes
Cooking time: 1 to 1½ hours
Serves 6

This potato dish is popular all over France—even throughout Europe. But when there are so many imitations, the goodness of the original taste tends to get lost. If you want to make a good version of this dish, choose the right potatoes, such as Yukon Gold, and a good-quality cream (don't use milk.)

PREHEAT THE OVEN to 375° F (190°C).

Peel and wash the potatoes and slice into ½-inch (1-cm) slices. Pat the potatoes dry. In a baking dish no deeper than 3 inches (8 cm), rub the surface with the cut garlic and a bit of the butter. Layer the potatoes, seasoning each layer with salt, pepper, and a pinch of grated nutmeg. Cover the potatoes entirely with the cream and dot the surface with pieces of butter. Bake in the preheated oven for 1 to 1½ hours, depending on the width of the gratin dish.

SUGGESTED WINES

Bordeaux Médoc, Château Sociando Mallet, France
or Osoyoos Larose, BC

The people of the north ("tc'hemi" to northern French locals) often use a mix of salt and sugar and have a characteristic slow cooking style. This recipe is a perfect example, as we pair the sweetness of apples and brown sugar with the saltiness of the cabbage. This makes a perfect starter or side dish for roasted goose, stuffed turkey, or venison.

Flemish Red Cabbage
CHOUX ROUGE À LA FLAMANDE

One 3-lb (1.5-kg) red cabbage

3 Tbsp (45 mL) lard or duck fat
(fine meat shop)

2 large onions, chopped

2 Tbsp (30 mL) brown sugar

Salt and pepper

Red wine

2 apples, peeled, cored and
cut into small cubes

Preparation time: 20 minutes
Cooking time: 40 minutes
Serves 6

DISCARD THE OUTER LEAVES of the red cabbage, cut out the core, rinse, cut into quarters and then into strips. Separate the cabbage layers.

In a large pot, heat the lard or duck fat over low heat and sauté the onions until they begin to brown, stirring often. Add the cabbage, brown sugar, salt, and pepper and mix well. Pour in enough red wine to come halfway up the vegetables. Cover and simmer at low heat for 30 minutes. Add the apple cubes, cover, and continue cooking for 30 minutes longer.

SUGGESTED WINES
Bordeaux Château Carignan, Bordeaux Supérieur, France
or Merlot collection, Tinhorn Creek, BC

This dessert is served cold. Use really nice pears with firm flesh, such as Anjou. You might want to accompany this dish with wine jelly or crème anglaise (see page 141) and place a few madeleines (see page 134) on the side.

Poached Pears in Red Wine and Spices
POIRES POCHÉES AU VIN ET ÉPICES

2 cups (500 mL) red wine

1 cup (250 mL) water

1 cup (250 mL) sugar

½ tsp (2 mL) cinnamon

1 whole clove

Freshly ground black pepper

6 Anjou pears

Preparation time: 20 minutes
Cooking time: 30 minutes
Serves 6

POUR THE WINE and water into a medium saucepan. Add the sugar, cinnamon, clove, and a pinch of pepper. Bring to a boil and reduce the heat.

Peel the pears, keeping them whole, and place them in the wine mixture. Cover and cook for 20 minutes at low heat. Remove the pears gently with a slotted spoon and place them in a shallow serving dish. Reduce the liquid to half and pour over the pears. Chill in the refrigerator for 1 hour before serving.

You can store the pears in syrup in an airtight container for up to 6 days in the refrigerator. Let the pears sit for 15 minutes at room temperature before serving.

SUGGESTED WINES
Selection Grains Nobles Riesling d'Ostertag, France
or Sequentia, Black Hills, BC

This is a traditional recipe from Brittany in northwestern France. It's an easy and fast dish to make. Just one thing to remember—don't refrigerate it or it will lose too much of its flavour. Cook it in the morning and leave it at room temperature until serving time.

Prune Clafoutis

FAR BRETON AUX PRUNEAUX ET VIN ROUGE

1 organic orange

1 cup (250 mL) red wine

1 cinnamon stick

1 whole clove

1 vanilla bean, split lengthwise, seeds removed

12 sugar cubes

15 dried prunes

4 cups (1 L) milk

6 egg yolks

½ cup (125 mL) sugar

½ cup (125 mL) custard powder

Preparation time: 20 minutes
Cooking time: 40 minutes
Serves 6

PUT A RACK AT THE LOWEST LEVEL OF THE OVEN and preheat to 450°F (230°C).

Remove the orange zest with a peeler and chop finely. In a saucepan, bring the wine to a boil. Add the orange zest, cinnamon stick, clove, vanilla pod halves and seeds, and sugar cubes. Cook for 5 minutes until the sugar has dissolved. Add the prunes and let cool at room temperature.

In another saucepan, bring the milk to a boil, then set aside. Combine the egg yolks and sugar in a bowl, whisking vigorously. Add the custard powder, pour in the hot milk, and mix well. Heat, cooking until thickened.

Pour the custard into an 8-inch (20-cm) pie pan. Top with the drained marinated prunes and bake in the preheated oven 35 to 40 minutes on the lowest rack. Let cool at room temperature and serve from the pie pan.

SUGGESTED WINES
Banyuls Cellier des Templiers, France
or Pipe, Sumac Ridge, BC

This dessert goes all the way back to 1891, honouring the year of the first Paris-Brest-Paris bicycle race. Said to be the first bicycle race ever held, it started in Paris, the riders following a route to the city of Brest on the Atlantic coast, then returning to the finish line in Paris. The circular form of this dessert is like a bicycle wheel.

Paris Brest

PARIS BREST

Confectioner's custard

2 cups (500 mL) milk

1 vanilla bean

6 egg yolks

½ cup (125 mL) sugar

¼ cup (60 mL) all-purpose flour

Butter

Choux pastry

1 cup (250 mL) milk

1 cup (250 mL) unsalted butter cut in pieces

1 cup (250 mL) all-purpose flour

2 tsp (10 mL) salt

2 tsp (10 mL) sugar

7 eggs

2 Tbsp (30 mL) sliced almonds

NOTE THAT THIS RECIPE IS FOR THE ADVANCED BAKER.

POUR THE MILK into a saucepan with the scraped seeds and the pods of the vanilla bean. Slowly bring to a boil and remove from the heat.

In a bowl, beat the egg yolks and sugar with a hand-held beater until the mixture whitens. Incorporate the flour and mix well. Incorporate the milk while beating continuously.

Pour the mixture into a clean pot and bring to a boil on low heat while continuously stirring, for 15 to 20 minutes. Remove from the heat and discard the vanilla pods. Melt a piece of butter over the surface of the custard with the help of a knife, so that a skin does not form. Cool completely, preferably overnight. (When it reaches room temperature, seal with plastic wrap, and keep in the refrigerator).

CHOUX PASTRY

Preheat the oven to 350°F (180°C). Put the milk, butter pieces, salt, and sugar in a medium-sized saucepan and bring to a boil on low heat. Remove from the heat and add the flour all at once to the boiling liquid. Mix vigorously with a wooden spoon. Put the pan back on low heat and continue mixing until the dough does not stick on the sides of the pot. Remove from the heat and incorporate the eggs one at the time, mixing vigorously with a wooden spoon after each egg.

Grease the inside of a 9-inch (1.5 L) round cake pan and transfer the dough to a pastry bag with a number 13 round tip (about ½ inch/1cm). Form the bottom layer by piping a crown of dough around the edges, then a second row just inside the first row. To form the second layer, pipe a row of dough on the seam between the 2 "rolls" from the first row. (A cross-section would look like 3 logs forming a triangle.) Sprinkle with sliced almonds. Bake in the preheated oven for 40 to 45 minutes. Leave the oven door slightly open after the first 15 minutes so that the dough dries well. Let cool at room temperature.

BUTTERCREAM

In a large bowl, mix the softened butter with the prepared custard with a hand-held mixer until nice and fluffy. Add the hazelnut paste to the custard mix and beat some more until smooth. Put the buttercream in a pastry bag with no tip.

TO ASSEMBLE

When the pastry crown is entirely cooled, slice it in two horizontally with the help of a serrated knife. Using a pastry bag with no tip, fill the hollow pastry bottom with the hazelnut buttercream and spread the filling evenly. Place the top part over the filled bottom and dust with powdered sugar just before serving. Use a serrated knife to cut pieces.

SUGGESTED WINES

Champagne Gosset, France
or Sparkling Wine, Sumac Ridge, BC

Buttercream

1 ½ cups (375 mL) softened unsalted butter

Confectioner's custard

½ cup (125 mL) or
¼ lb (125 g) hazelnut paste
(order from a fine pastry shop)

Preparation time: 1 ½ hours
(it's better to make the custard
a day ahead)
Cooking time: 45 minutes
Serves 4 to 6

This recipe comes with a story. At the end of the 19th century, Fanny Tatin and her sister owned a hotel near the train station at Lamotte Beuvron, in the region of Sologne. One day, ready to put a pie in the oven, Fanny fell and the pie ended upside down on the ground. Instead of throwing it out, she decided to cook it that way, and serve it inverted. Her good idea and quick thinking was the beginning of the dessert called Tarte Tatin. For the best tarte, use apples that are tender and a little sweet. And be careful. Caramel can cause bad burns, so use oven mitts when you're dealing with it.

Tarte Tatin

TARTE TATIN

½ cup (125 mL) sugar

¼ cup (60 mL) unsalted butter

6–7 apples, peeled, cored, and quartered

1 sheet frozen puff pastry
(thaw according to package instructions)

Preparation time: 30 minutes
Cooking time: 50 minutes
Serves 4 to 6

PREHEAT THE OVEN to 400°F (200°C).

To make the caramel, mix the sugar and butter in a cast-iron mould or an ovenproof 8-inch (20-cm) round pan. Cook over medium heat for 15 minutes, until golden brown. Swirl the caramel so that it covers the bottom of the pan. Arrange the apples cut-side down, packing them tightly in a neat pattern on the caramel. Bake in the preheated oven for 1 hour. Remove the pan from the oven and let it cool.

Roll the puff pastry ⅛ inch (3 mm) thick and cut a circle slightly larger than your baking dish. Place the pastry on top of the apples and tuck the edges inside the pan. Bake in the oven for another 30 minutes until the pastry is cooked. Let cool to room temperature.

Place a serving dish on top and carefully invert the tarte and serving dish together. Remove the pan and serve the tarte warm with a dab of whipped cream or vanilla ice cream.

SUGGESTED WINES
Côteaux du Layon, Château de Fesles, France
or Sequentia, Black Hills, BC

TARTE TATIN
PAGE 96

BLUE CHEESE AND PEAR TART

PAGE 75

SAFFRON AND CHORIZO
HALIBUT BOULANGÈRE
PAGE 78

ORANGE CAKE
PAGE 98

There are two types of acidity in this recipe, the Granny Smith apples and the rhubarb. I like very much the contrast between the two textures. You can use frozen rhubarb from the supermarket, but you can easily find fresh rhubarb until late November. If you want, add one small spoonful of finely chopped rosemary in the last ten minutes of cooking. This will make a different dessert—but one that's very tasty too.

Rhubarb and Apple Compote
COMPOTE DE RHUBARBE ET POMMES

5 Granny Smith apples, peeled, cored and chopped

1 lb (500 g) rhubarb, washed, peeled and chopped

2 vanilla beans, split lengthwise, seeds removed

2 Tbsp (30 mL) unsalted butter

½ cup (125 mL) water

½ cup (125 mL) sugar

Preparation time: 20 minutes
Cooking time: 20 minutes
Serves 6

PLACE THE APPLES, rhubarb, and vanilla pods and seeds in a heavy-bottomed pot. Add the butter, water, and sugar. Cook over medium heat for 30 minutes. Remove from the stove, remove the vanilla pods, and let cool. Refrigerate before serving.

This sauce is delicious served with vanilla ice cream and a few madeleines (see page 134). Keeps in an airtight container for up to a week.

SUGGESTED WINES
Jurancon Domaine du Cinquau, France
or Sparkling Riesling Ice Wine, Jackson Triggs, BC

Orange Cake

GÂTEAU À L'ORANGE

This recipe calls for biscuit dough, which is light and ideal for cold or frozen fruit-based desserts. Smooth and supple, the cooked dough won't crumble or crack in the refrigerator or freezer.

Biscuit Dough

4 whole eggs, separated

½ cup (125 mL) sugar

4 egg yolks

⅔ cup (160 mL) flour

BISCUIT DOUGH

IN A LARGE BOWL, beat the egg whites with a hand-held mixer, folding in half the sugar a little bit at a time, until firm peaks form. In another bowl, beat the 8 egg yolks and the remaining sugar until the yolks are pale and frothy.

With a wooden spoon, fold the yolk mixture into the egg whites little by little. When the egg yolks are incorporated, dust the mixture with some flour, fold it in, and continue adding a little at a time until it's all incorporated.

Orange cake

Preheat the oven to 350°F (180°C).

Melt the butter. Using a pastry brush, butter the sides of an 8-inch (20-cm) charlotte mould and dust generously with powdered sugar. Pour the biscuit dough into the mould, filling it two-thirds full.

Bake for 40 minutes. The cake is done when the blade of a thin knife or a bamboo skewer comes out clean when inserted deep into the middle of the cake. Unmould on a cake rack and let cool.

Cut the cake into two equal layers. Thin out the orange syrup with the water and moisten the first layer of cake. Spread the marmalade evenly, place the other cake layer on top, and moisten lightly with orange syrup. Mix the fondant with the orange liqueur, if desired, and spread evenly on top of the cake. Decorate the cake artfully with orange slices.

Suggested wines
Champagne Pommery, France
or Méthode Champenoise Brut, Sumac Ridge

Orange Cake

1 ½ Tbsp (20 mL) butter

2 Tbsp (30 mL) powdered sugar

Biscuit dough

½ cup (125 mL) orange syrup

¼ cup (60 mL) water

1 cup (250 mL) orange marmalade

⅓ lb (170 g) fondant,
found in fine pastry supply shop
(optional)

1 ½ Tbsp (20 ml) curaçao
or orange liqueur (optional)

1 organic seedless orange,
thinly sliced

Preparation: 45 minutes
Cooking time: 40 minutes
Serves 4 to 6

Winter

Winter for me means rejoicing with good friends close to a fire in an old rustic fireplace, sharing a decadent braised meal like a pot-au-feu or a cassoulet and a good bottle of wine. Here I propose an old fondue recipe of Swiss origin, very simple and very good:

"Take the amount of eggs you want to use, according to the amount of guests, then measure up grated Gruyère to a third of that weight and a piece of butter a sixth of that weight. Whisk the eggs in a shallow pot, and add Gruyère and butter. At medium heat, stir constantly over the stove with a wooden spoon until the mixture thickens. Add a pinch of pepper."

When I was a young boy, my grandmother would prepare a winter version of her red wine soup for the children, and it would be warm and flavoured with freshly ground spices, and served with burned bread.

Another tradition in France is *la fête des rois*, or Épiphanie, celebrated on January 6. Épiphanie means "manifestation," or "appearance of a divinity" in Greek. This was the day when the three wise men first beheld the Christ child, and the day He was baptized. On that day, a galette, a flat cake, was served with a black bean inserted in the dough before cooking. There was one portion per guest, and one extra for an unannounced guest. If you found the bean in your piece, you'd be king for the day!

This was my favourite soup after a booming night out on the town.

Baked French Onion Soup

GRATINÉE À L'OIGNON

½ cup (125 mL) unsalted butter

4 large yellow onions, minced

8 cups (2 L) chicken stock

1 stale baguette

24 fine slices Gruyère cheese

3 egg yolks (optional)

¼ cup (60 mL) port
(optional)

Preparation time: 25 minutes
Cooking time: 10 to 15 minutes
Serves 6

IN A WIDE, HEAVY-BOTTOMED POT, melt the butter at medium-low heat and sauté the onions for 15 minutes or until they're lightly coloured. Pour the stock over the onions, bring to a boil, reduce the heat, and simmer for 10 minutes.

Slice the baguette into ¼-inch (5-mm) slices and grill on both sides under the broiler until golden.

Preheat the oven to 350°F (180°C).

Place the croutons in individual ovenproof soup crocks and cover with 2 slices of cheese. Ladle the soup on top and add the remaining croutons and 2 slices of cheese on top. Place the crocks on a baking sheet and bake in preheated oven for 10 to 15 minutes, until the cheese on top is crispy.

OPTIONAL

Beat 3 egg yolks with a glass of port and pour under the cheesy crust when you remove the soup from the oven.

SUGGESTED WINES
Riesling, Hugel, France
or Riesling, Saturna Island Vineyards, BC

If possible, use the French green lentils from Puy. They're more flavourful, and their longer cooking time allows the other vegetables to cook to perfection. This is another wonderful soup for a cool winter night spent by the fire with friends or family.

Lentil Cream Soup with Bacon

CRÈME DE LENTILLES ET BACON

2 cups (500 mL) lentils

1 carrot,
cut in large chunks

1 onion,
cut in large chunks

1 bouquet garni (see page 138)

4 thick slices bacon

2 cups (500 mL) whipping cream

Salt and pepper

Preparation time: 30 minutes
Cooking time: 30 minutes
Serves 4

PLACE THE LENTILS in a pot filled with cold water and bring to a boil. Boil the lentils uncovered for a few seconds, drain, and transfer to a pot filled with cold water. Add the carrot, onion, and bouquet garni. Cover and cook on low heat for 25 minutes.

Fry the bacon slices and place on paper towels to absorb the excess fat.

Once the lentils are cooked, discard the vegetable chunks and bouquet garni. Drain the lentils, keeping the cooking liquid. Purée the lentils in a blender, adding some cooking liquid to liquefy the purée. Strain the purée through a sieve with the help of a wooden spoon. Pour the purée into a pot and add some more cooking liquid. Incorporate the cream and bring to a boil. Correct the seasoning and blend once again, either in the food processor or with a hand-held mixer, for an unctuous texture.

Serve the soup in shallow soup plates and garnish with a slice of crispy bacon. You can also garnish with fried flat-leaf parsley.

SUGGESTED WINES
Madiran Château Montus, France
or Cabernet Sauvignon, Fairview Cellars, BC

This is the perfect example of French bourgeois cooking. Serve it a little warm, with a spoonful of melted butter and a nice side salad.

Pâté en Croûte

PÂTÉ EN CROÛTE

Filling

1 Tbsp (15 mL) unsalted butter

2 carrots, chopped

4 shallots, chopped

One 3–4-lb (1.5–2-kg) organic chicken, skin and bones removed

5 oz (150 g) pork loin

5 oz (150 g) pork leg slice

5 oz (150 g) veal round

½ lb (250 g) unsmoked slab bacon, diced

1 sprig parsley

8–10 whole black peppercorns

½ cup (125 mL) Madeira

4 cups (1 L) chicken stock

THE DAY BEFORE

FILLING

THE DAY BEFORE SERVING, heat the butter in a pan and sauté the carrots and shallots for 3 or 4 minutes. Set aside in a large bowl.

Remove the tendons from the chicken thighs and cut the thighs, pork, veal, and bacon into large cubes. Cut the remaining chicken meat into thin strips. Mix the meat with the vegetables and add the parsley and whole peppercorns. Pour in the Madeira and 2 cups (500 mL) of the chicken stock, cover with plastic wrap and refrigerate overnight.

CRUST

Place the flour, salt, and butter in the food processor with the plastic blade. Add the eggs and knead rapidly, adding the water by drops until the dough forms a ball. Transfer the dough to a sheet of plastic wrap. Use the plastic to gather it into a ball, seal it, and refrigerate overnight.

THE NEXT DAY

TO FINISH

Preheat the oven to 475°F (230°C).

Place the foie gras in lukewarm water for 2 minutes to soften. Drain and separate the lobes so that you can remove the nerves with the help of a paring knife. Season the foie gras with salt and pepper and form it into a sausage shape.

Take the dough out of the refrigerator, and allow it to reach room temperature. Drain the meat pieces from the marinade and set the chicken strips on a separate dish. Cut the pieces of meat into smaller cubes and season with salt and pepper.

Melt the butter in a small pan and sear the foie gras on all sides over high heat. Set aside. Grind the marinated meats and cubed slab bacon together to form a chunky filling (if you don't have a meat grinder, use a food processor, grinding a few pieces at a time with short pulses to make sure that you don't over-grind). Place the meat in a large bowl. Mix in the Madeira and lightly beaten eggs and stir vigorously. Set aside.

On a floured surface, roll three-quarters of the dough into a rectangle ¼ inch (5 mm) thick, to cover the inside of your terrine. Roll the remaining dough into a rectangle a bit larger than the top of the terrine.

Grease an 8 x 4-inch (20 x 10-cm/1.5-L) ceramic terrine or loaf pan and lay the dough on the bottom and up the sides. Line the dough with a layer of fatback, reserving some for the top. Place half the filling inside and lay the strips of chicken on top. Add the foie gras and then the rest of the filling in layers. The filling can be heaped in the terrine. Finish with the remaining fatback, and cover the pâté with a layer of dough, pinching the edges together to make it airtight. Brush the dough with a beaten egg yolk. Cut 2 dime-sized holes in the dough to let steam escape.

Cook in the preheated oven for 15 minutes, then reduce the heat to 375°F (190°C) and cook for 1 hour and 15 minutes longer. Remove from the oven and let rest for at least 20 minutes. Serve warm.

SUGGESTED WINES
Mercurey Domaine Michel Julliot, France
or Pinot Noir, Blue Mountain, BC

Crust

3½ cups (875 mL) all-purpose flour

1 tsp (5 mL) salt

1½ cups (375 mL) unsalted butter, cut into cubes

2 eggs

2–3 Tbsp (30–45 mL) water

To Finish

1-lb (500-g) piece of fresh foie gras

Salt and pepper

1 Tbsp (15 mL) unsalted butter

½ cup (125 mL) Madeira

2 eggs, lightly beaten

8–10 slices fatback or caul fat (ask your butcher)

1 egg yolk (for glazing)

The day before:
prepare the vegetables, meats, marinade, and dough.
Preparation time: 1 hour
Cooking time: 1½ hours
Serves 10

Escargots are certainly a symbolic food of French cuisine. I use the more tender small grey ones. I suggest avoiding snails farmed in China, as they're very rubbery. Fresh snails are better than canned, though they demand more time and determination. Should you accept this mission ... I recommend cooking the snails and preparing the escargot butter the previous day, leaving only about 3 hours of preparation the following day. This is the French way!

Escargots and Tomato Confit Bake
CROÛTON D'ESCARGOTS

Live Snails

3 dozen petits gris live snails (Note: If you use canned or bottled snails, they need no cooking and are added in the final baking stage. Therefore, omit the next 8 ingredients)

Water

Salt

3 cups (750 mL) dry white wine

3 cups (750 mL) water

½ carrot

½ onion

5 shallots, halved

Bouquet garni (see page 138)

2 tsp (10 mL) salt

NOTE: IF YOU WANT TO PREPARE AND COOK LIVE SNAILS (OR JUST EXPAND YOUR CULINARY KNOWLEDGE) READ ON. IF YOU ARE USING CANNED OR BOTTLED SNAILS, SKIP TO THE TOMATO CONCASSÉ.

LIVE SNAILS

PLACE THE SNAILS in a bowl and wash with water. Repeat the washing process a few times, with fresh water each time. In the same bowl, cover the snails with water and add some salt. Soak for 3 to 4 hours, then rinse thoroughly again.

Place the snails in a large pot, cover with fresh water and bring the water to a boil. Lower the heat to a simmer and blanch for 5 minutes. In a colander, drain the snails and rinse with cold water.

Using a fork, twist the snails free of their shells, and discard the black spiral located at the top of the shell. Return to the pot, adding the wine, water, vegetables, bouquet garni and salt. Bring to a boil and simmer gently on low heat for 4 hours. Let them cool in the cooking water. Discard the vegetables, drain the snails, and set aside (seal with a wrap and refrigerate if using the following day).

continues on next page

Tomato Concassé

20 medium-sized ripe tomatoes

Sea salt (preferably *fleur de sel*) and pepper

Powdered sugar

⅔ cup + 2 Tbsp (100 mL) virgin olive oil

Escargot Butter

½ lb (225 g) unsalted butter

2 cloves garlic

½ bunch Italian parsley, stems removed

2 Tbsp (30 mL) old-fashioned French mustard

2 Tbsp (30 mL) ground almonds

1 tsp (5 mL) salt

¼ cup (60 mL) finely chopped white mushrooms

¼ cup (60 mL) finely chopped prosciutto

3 Tbsp (45 mL) shallots, minced

TOMATO CONCASSÉ

Put the tomatoes in a bowl of boiling water for a few seconds. Slip off the skins, cut the tomatoes in quarters, remove the cores and seeds, and drain. Keep only the outer flesh, now resembling petals.

Keep about 6 of the tomatoes (or 24 petals) intact, plus 4 petals for later use as garnish, and finely chop (concassé) the remaining petals.

Preheat the oven to 225°F (105°C).

Place the 24 petals and the concassé in a medium bowl and add salt and pepper. Dust with powdered sugar, add olive oil, and mix well. Pour the tomato mix in a Dutch oven and bring to a boil. Reduce heat to medium and let the tomatoes sweat. When their cooking juices rise to the surface, transfer the pot to the oven and cook uncovered for 2½ hours, until the liquid has completely evaporated. The tomatoes will have the consistency of compote. Set aside in the casserole and increase the oven temperature up to 350°F (180°C).

ESCARGOT BUTTER

Put all the ingredients in a food processor and mix until you obtain a fine butter. If making on the same day, leave at room temperature. If making the day before serving, store in the refrigerator and take out 2 hours before using.

GARNISH

Clean, drain and pat dry 4 sprigs of parsley. In a small pan, pour about 1 inch (2.5 cm) of vegetable oil and bring to about 375°F (190°C) on your deep-fryer thermometer. Cut the parsley stems off, then drop leaves in the oil for a few seconds, until crisp. Gently scoop out the parsley with a metal slotted spoon, drain on paper towels and set aside.

While your oil is heating up, melt the butter over a bain-marie or in a microwave-safe dish. Skim off any foam and pour the clear liquid off the solids that collect on the bottom.

Use a bit of the clarified butter to brush the bread slices. On a cooking sheet, bake the 4 croutons until crisp but not coloured. Set aside.

To finish

Place the warm tomato confit at the bottom of four individual ceramic serving dishes. Coat the escargots with a bit of clarified butter and place 8 escargots (keep the 9th one aside for garnish) on each bed of tomato confit. Cover with escargot butter. (You will need to use about ¾ of the quantity you made. You can freeze the remaining butter for later use).

Gently push the croutons on top of the escargots, covering the dish like dough, and bake for about 10–15 minutes until the croutons are golden brown and the butter bubbly. Before serving, cut the remaining 4 tomato petals into thin slices, and spread artfully on each crouton. Quickly warm up the 4 remaining escargots and place in the centre, and garnish with fried parsley. Voila!

Suggested wines

Chablis de chez Moreau, France
or Chardonnay, Seven Poplars, Lake Breeze, BC

Garnish

4 parsley sprigs

Vegetable oil for deep-frying

4 slices bread,
large enough to cover
individual ceramic serving dishes

½ lb (250 g) butter

Preparation time: 7 hours
(if using live snails)
Cooking time: 3 hours
Serves 4

People forget about wonderful meat terrines these days. It's too bad, because they're easy to make and full of flavour. The basic ingredient is the same for all meat terrines: start with good, finely ground pork. "Vive le cochon," and dust off your ceramic terrines!

Country-Style Terrine

PÂTÉ DE CAMPAGNE

Chicken Livers and Marinade

1 lb (500 g) chicken livers

2 tsp (10 mL) port

4 tsp (20 mL) cognac

2 tsp (10 mL) sherry

1 clove garlic, crushed

1 tsp (5 mL) sea salt

1 tsp (5 mL) freshly ground pepper

½ tsp (2 mL) allspice

Pinch dried thyme

Pinch minced dried parsley

CHICKEN LIVERS AND MARINADE

MARINATE THE CHICKEN LIVERS in the port, cognac, sherry, garlic, salt, pepper, allspice, and dried herbs for 1 hour. Strain through a sieve and keep the marinade in the refrigerator for later. Cut the livers into strips and set aside.

GROUND PORK MIXTURE

Mix the ground pork with the salt, pepper, garlic, thyme, port, cognac, and sherry. Mix in the chicken liver strips and the reserved marinade.

TO ASSEMBLE

Preheat the oven to 475°F (240°C).

Line a 4 x 8-inch (10 x 20-cm/1.5-L) ceramic terrine with fatback slices and place 2 bay leaves on the bottom. Fill the terrine with the filling and pack down well by tapping the dish on the counter. Cover the terrine with the remaining fatback or caul fat and place 3 bay leaves on top. Cover tightly with aluminum foil or the terrine lid. Place the terrine in a larger ovenproof dish and put enough water to come halfway up the sides of the terrine. Cook in the bain-marie in the preheated oven for 3 hours. The pâté is cooked when you insert a knife in the middle for 20 seconds and the blade is hot all along.

Once cooked, remove lid and place a heavy weight on top of the foil to press the meat. Remove the fat and juices rising to the surface. With the weight on, let the terrine stand to cool, then refrigerate for 36 hours. Serve with pickles and/or pickled vegetables and large slices of toasted country bread.

SUGGESTED WINES
Sancerre Rouge Lucien Crochet, France
or Cabernet Franc, Fairview Cellars, BC

Ground Pork Mixture

1 lb (500 g) ground pork

1½ Tbsp (20 mL) sea salt

1 tsp (5 mL) freshly ground pepper

1 clove garlic, chopped

Pinch thyme

1 tsp (5 mL) port

1 tsp (5 mL) cognac

1 tsp (5 mL) sherry

10–12 thin slices fatback or caul fat
(ask your butcher)

5 bay leaves

Preparation time: 2 hours
Cooking time: 3 hours
Resting time: 36 hours
Serves 15

A few ham hocks, one or two veal feet for the gelatin, Dijon mustard, parsley—this dish has all the attributes of typical Burgundy cooking. When I can pair this dish with a glass of Morgon from my friend Jean Foillard's vineyard, I'm in paradise.

Ham and Parsley Aspic

JAMBON PERSILLÉ

2 ham hocks, bone in

1 veal foot, cut in half
(ask your butcher)

2 carrots, cubed

1 whole onion

2 whole cloves

1 bouquet garni (see page 138)

5 whole black peppercorns

6 shallots

4 cloves garlic

1 bunch flat-leaf parsley,
rinsed and dried

2 Tbsp (30 mL) Dijon mustard

2 Tbsp (30 mL) red wine vinegar

1 tsp (5 mL) allspice

Nutmeg

Salt and pepper

Preparation time: 30 minutes
Cooking time: 2½ hours
Resting time: 24 hours
Serves 8 to 10

THE DAY BEFORE

IN A LARGE POT, place the ham and veal foot. Add the carrots, the onion pricked with whole cloves, the bouquet garni, and peppercorns. Cover with cold water. Bring to a boil, and simmer at low heat for 2½ hours, skimming the fat off the surface.

Peel and finely chop the shallots and garlic. Finely chop the parsley then mix with the shallots and garlic. Add the mustard, vinegar, and allspice, and grate a pinch of nutmeg over. Season with salt and pepper. Set aside.

When the meat is cooked, remove it from the pot and set aside. Strain the cooking liquid through a fine sieve and discard the vegetables. Finely chop the veal. Remove the bones from the hocks and chop the meat into large cubes. Line any size or shape of terrine with plastic wrap. Place the meat inside and pour the shallot and parsley mixture on top, shaking the terrine to ensure that the mixture slides between the ham cubes and veal. Add 4 to 5 ladles of cooking liquid. Tap the terrine on the counter to ensure that the liquid coats the ham cubes. Cover the terrine with plastic wrap and refrigerate for 24 hours.

THE NEXT DAY

Transfer the terrine to a cutting board and gently slice with a serrated knife dipped in hot water between every cut, or better yet, an electric knife. Serve with pickles and Dijon mustard.

SUGGESTED WINES

Morgon Jean Foillard, France
or Gamay, Stag's Hollow, BC

This is very "centre-of-France" regional cooking. In Lyon it's a typical dish served at that most important family meal, Sunday lunch.

Cod Dumplings Lyonnaise

QUENELLES DE MORUE À LA LYONNAISE

Sauce

2 Tbsp (30 mL) canola oil

2 lb (1 kg) chicken bones

1 Tbsp (15 mL) unsalted butter

1 carrot, cut in
1-inch (2.5-cm) pieces

1 onion, cut in
1-inch (2.5-cm) pieces

1 leek, cleaned,
white part cut in large slices

2 Tbsp (30 mL) tomato paste

2 Tbsp (30 mL) all-purpose flour

Water

1 bouquet garni (see page 138)

3 tomatoes

12 medium-sized green olives,
pitted and chopped

SAUCE

HEAT THE OIL IN A PAN and sear the chicken bones over medium-high heat.

In a large pot, heat the butter and sauté the carrot, onion, and leek for 5 minutes. Stir in the tomato paste and cook a few minutes more. Sprinkle with flour and add the seared chicken bones. Add enough water to cover and add the bouquet garni. Bring to a boil, then reduce the heat and simmer for 1 ½ hours. Meanwhile, put the tomatoes in a bowl of water for a few seconds, slip off the skins, cut in quarters, remove the seeds, and drain. Cut again in cubes and set aside. When the sauce is cooked, strain through a fine sieve into a bowl and discard all solids. Add the sliced green olives and set aside.

DUMPLINGS

Pour the milk into a saucepan and add the butter. Season with salt, white pepper, and a pinch of freshly grated nutmeg. Bring to a boil then add the flour all at once, stirring vigorously with a wooden spoon. Dry out the dough, ensuring that it does not stick to the sides of the pot. Remove from the heat and incorporate 3 of the eggs, one at the time, beating vigorously to incorporate each egg before adding the next. Refrigerate to cool.

Place the cod meat in the food processor, season with salt, pepper, and a pinch of grated nutmeg. Purée the fish, whipping cream, and the 2 remaining eggs together. When the dough has cooled down, incorporate the fish purée into the dough with a wooden spoon. Return to the refrigerator.

When you're ready to shape the dumplings, set a bowl of cold water beside you. With wet hands, form the mixture into rounded football shapes (about 4 inches/10 cm long) and set on parchment or waxed paper. Bring a large pot of water to a boil and poach the dumplings for 15 to 20 minutes in simmering water. The dumplings are cooked when they rise to the surface. Transfer the cooked dumplings to a bowl of cold water for about 5 minutes to stop the cooking process. Remove the dumplings with a slotted spoon, and drain on a clean cloth. When dry, place them in a shallow dish. They can be baked now or held, covered with plastic wrap, until later.

GARNISH

Preheat the oven to 500°F (260°C).

In a pan over medium heat, cook the mushrooms in the butter and lemon juice for 10 minutes. Add the mushrooms and cubed tomatoes to the sauce, coat the dumplings, and bake in the preheated oven for 15 minutes (you'll see them puff up).

SUGGESTED WINES
Macon Blanc, Jean Thevenet, France
or Chardonnay, Saturna Island, BC

Dumplings

1 cup (250 mL) milk

⅓ cup (80 mL) unsalted butter

Salt and white pepper

Freshly grated nutmeg

¾ cup (180 mL) all-purpose flour

5 eggs

½ lb (500 g) cod fillets

Salt and white pepper

Nutmeg

3 Tbsp (45 mL) whipping cream

Garnish

½ lb (500 g) white mushrooms, sliced

2 Tbsp (30 mL) unsalted butter

1 Tbsp (15 mL) lemon juice
(about ½ lemon)

Preparation time: 1 hour
Cooking time: 15 minutes
Serves 4

Stuffed Cabbage

CHOUX FARÇI

1 large head savoy cabbage
(curly leaves)

1 bunch chard, washed

1 lb (500 g) pork fat,
cut in small cubes

1 clove garlic

3 shallots

12 sprigs flat-leaf parsley

12 sprigs chervil

¼ cup (60 mL) buckwheat flour

1 cup (250 mL) whipping cream

10 eggs

Salt and pepper

Nutmeg

4–6 slices fatback, or caul fat
(ask your butcher)

3 medium carrots, peeled,
washed, and thinly sliced

Preparation time: 45 minutes
Cooking time: 2 hours
Serves 4

Cabbage is a perfect vegetable to use in slow-cooked winter dishes. Its leaves absorb all the flavours of the ingredients it is cooked with. For instance, cook it with butter and it will take the flavour of the butter. Cook with foie gras, and it will soak in all the flavour of the foie gras. This dish is a regional recipe from Auvergne in France.

CORE THE CABBAGE and discard the outer leaves. Separate the leaves and wash thoroughly. Remove the thick centre rib of each leaf. Place the cabbage leaves in a large pot and cover with cold water. Bring to a boil over low heat. Drain and place on a clean cloth to dry.

Remove the leaves from the chard stems, peel the stems on both sides, and cut in pieces. In a pot, boil some water, add the stem pieces, and cook for 5 minutes. Add the leaves and cook for 2 minutes longer, then drain. Set aside. In the same pot, boil more water and blanch the pork fat cubes for about 30 seconds and drain.

Roughly chop the chard, pork fat, garlic, shallots, parsley, and chervil. Combine in a large bowl and stir in the buckwheat flour. Add the cream, then stir in the eggs, one at a time, always stirring in the same direction (this process helps to incorporate the eggs). Season with salt, pepper, and grated nutmeg.

Cut some kitchen string into eight 24-inch (60-cm) lengths. Drape the string pieces over the bottom of a 9-inch (23-cm/1.5-L) round ceramic terrine so that they cross in a starburst in the centre, with the ends hanging over the sides. Line the terrine with the fatback or caul fat. Cover the bottom with a layer of half the sliced carrots. Line the terrine with the largest cabbage leaves, first going up the sides and over, then with a layer of cabbage leaves over the carrots. Set aside.

Preheat the oven to 425°F (220°C).

Coat the bottom with a ½-inch (1-cm) layer of the chard mixture, then alternate with a layer of cabbage leaves. Finish with a layer of cabbage. Fold in the outer cabbage leaves to seal. Arrange the remaining carrot slices before covering with remaining fatback slices or the caul. Tie the opposite strings together to insure a cabbagelike shape. Seal tightly with aluminum foil. Cook in the preheated oven for 2 hours. When cooked, discard the foil and pour the liquid out before transferring onto a cutting board. Remove the strings and cut the stuffed cabbage into slices, just like a cake.

SUGGESTED WINES

Saint Joseph Rouge, Pierre Gaillard, France
or Syrah, Nichol Vineyard, BC

I FAIL TO SEE HOW THIS "BUILDS CHARACTER"!

This recipe requires long, slow cooking. It's possible to make it on two separate days—the flavour is better the second day. One bit of advice: when you place the ovenproof dish in the oven, invert the lid and fill the hollow part with water. This will provide more even cooking. Serve with mashed potatoes (page 41). Yummy!

Beef Bourguignon
BOEUF BOURGUIGNON

¾ cup (180 mL) canola oil

¾ cup (180 mL) unsalted butter

3 lb (1.5 kg) beef brisket, cut in 2-inch (5-cm) cubes

3 medium carrots, minced

2 onions, minced

2 cloves garlic, crushed

3 Tbsp (45 mL) all-purpose flour

3 cups (750 mL) Pinot Noir (preferably Burgundy)

¼ cup (60 mL) beef stock

Salt and pepper

1 bouquet garni (see page 138)

½ lb (500 g) bacon, chopped

½ lb (500 g) white mushrooms, wiped clean, cut in quarters

40 pearl onions, peeled and rinsed

Sugar

2 Tbsp chopped flat-leaf parsley

Preparation time: 25 minutes
Cooking time: 2 to 3 hours
Serves 8

IN A DUTCH OVEN, heat some of the oil and butter. Sear the meat, a few pieces at the time, until well browned. Set the pieces aside and heat more oil and butter before searing the next pieces. When all the meat is done, sauté the carrots, onions, and garlic in the same pot. Stir for about 10 minutes, until soft and golden.

Turn on the broiler. Return the meat to the pot and mix with the vegetables. Sprinkle the flour over, mixing well. Place uncovered in the oven, allowing the flour to brown (about 5 minutes). Remove from the oven and set aside.

Adjust the oven temperature to 400°F (200°C).

Pour in the wine and beef stock, making sure to scrape the bottom of the pot with a wooden spoon. Season with salt and pepper and add the bouquet garni. Cover and cook for 2½ hours, stirring every 20 to 25 minutes, making sure to scrape the bottom of the pot.

While the meat is braising, sauté the bacon in a large frying pan. Transfer to paper towels, pat dry, and set aside. Remove all but a spoonful of the bacon fat and sauté the mushrooms. Drain and set aside with the bacon. Add the remaining butter, the pearl onions, a bit of sugar, and enough water to cover the bottom of the pan. Cover and simmer until the water has evaporated. Remove from the heat and let rest in the pan.

When the meat is cooked, skim off any surface fat and check the seasoning. Stir in the bacon, mushrooms, and onions. Serve in shallow plates and finish with chopped parsley.

SUGGESTED WINES
Châteauneuf du Pape, Domaine de Beaucastel, France
or Syrah, La Frenz, BC

This must be close to a record for slow cooking! We're a very long way from the al dente *vegetables we're now used to cooking. Beautiful bright colours—but we sometimes forget that braising really brings out the flavours. Serve this dish with a spoon; you don't need a knife because the meat is so tender.*

Seven-Hour Leg of Lamb

GIGOT D'AGNEAU SEPT HEURES

2 Tbsp (30 mL) canola oil

One 4–5-lb (2–2.2-kg) boneless leg of lamb (ask your butcher)

2 onions, peeled, washed, and cut in small cubes

1 head garlic, cloves separated, peeled, and crushed

2 carrots, peeled, washed, and cut in small cubes

3 cups (750 mL) lamb stock (fine food markets)

½ lb (500 g) pork skin (optional, ask your butcher)

A few sprigs thyme

3 bay leaves

2 Tbsp (30 mL) tomato paste

1 cup (250 mL) white wine

Salt and pepper

Preparation time: 30 minutes
Cooking time: 7 hours
Serves 8

HEAT HALF OF THE OIL in a Dutch oven and sear the lamb on all sides. When seared, rest the lamb on a plate. In the same pot, heat the remaining oil and cook the onions, crushed garlic cloves, and carrots until they are golden brown. Remove the vegetables from the pot and set aside on a plate.

Preheat the oven to 200°F (95°C).

Heat the stock in a saucepan. Cover the bottom of the Dutch oven with the pork skin and place the leg of lamb on it. Add the reserved vegetables, thyme, bay leaves, tomato paste, white wine, and warm stock. Season with salt and pepper. Cook in preheated oven for 7 hours.

With a ladle, transfer the gravy into a sauce dish. Present the lamb in the stewing pot and serve it on hot, shallow plates with spoons.

SUGGESTED WINES
Pomerol, Vieux Château-Certan, France
or Meritage, Jackson Triggs, BC

This is a real French country dish whose name doesn't even translate into English. It has many intense flavours and it's very rich—savour it in moderation. The dish varies from village to village; in some places they add currants and chopped hard-boiled eggs to the stuffing. You need time to make this recipe and you have to pay attention when simmering. It's also helpful to have all the ingredients chopped, measured, and ready in separate piles, because you'll be taking portions of them as you go along.

La Falette

LA FALETTE

2 slices bread, crust removed

½ cup (125 mL) milk

¼ lb (125 g) ground pork

¼ lb (125 g) spinach leaves, washed and chopped

¼ lb (125 g) chard, washed and chopped

4 cloves garlic, crushed

3 onions, chopped

1 small bunch parsley, chopped

Salt and pepper

One 3–4-lb (1.5–2-kg) boneless breast of lamb

2 Tbsp (30 mL) unsalted butter

1 carrot, cut into ¼-inch (5-mm) cubes

SOAK THE BREAD in the milk then squeeze it to drain. In a bowl, mix the drained bread with the ground pork, spinach, chard, one-third of the crushed garlic, one-third of the chopped onion and all the parsley until well blended. Season with salt and pepper. Lay the lamb breast flat on a chopping board and season with salt and pepper. Place the stuffing mix in the middle, roll up, and tie the roll with string.

Preheat the oven to 350°F (180°C).

In a Dutch oven, heat 1 Tbsp (15 mL) of the butter and sear the meat on all sides for a few minutes. Remove and set aside. Add the remaining butter to the pot and sauté half the carrot and celery, one-third of the chopped onions, and one-third of the crushed garlic for a few minutes. Place the lamb on top of the vegetables, pour in the white wine and half of the chicken stock, and add the thyme and bay leaf. Cover and braise in the oven for 1 hour and 45 minutes.

Meanwhile, put the tomatoes in boiling water for a few seconds, remove the skins, seed, drain, and chop. In a large pot, sauté the cubed ham with the remaining garlic, onions, celery, and carrots. A few minutes later add the chopped tomatoes and mix well. Add the bouquet garni and white beans. Pour the remaining stock over top and add some hot water, if necessary, to cover the beans. Cover and simmer for 1 hour, until the beans are tender.

When the lamb roast is cooked, remove from the dish, discard the string, slice, and place on a hot serving dish. Garnish with the bean mixture. Strain and reduce the cooking juices, check the seasoning and serve on the side as a sauce.

SUGGESTED WINES
Château Le Tertre Rôteboeuf, St-Émilion, France
or Reserve, Fairview Cellars, BC

1 stalk celery, cut into ¼-inch (5-mm) cubes

1 cup (250 mL) white wine

1 ½ cups (375 mL) chicken stock

2 sprigs thyme

1 bay leaf

3 tomatoes

¼ lb (125 g) thick slice ham, cut in small cubes

1 bouquet garni (see page 138)

1 lb (500 g) white beans (soaked for a minimum of 3 hours in cold water)

Preparation time: 50 minutes
Cooking time: 1¾ hrs
Serves 6

Pot-au-feu

POT-AU-FEU

½ lb (250 g) beef bones

3 lb (1.5 kg) beef shanks

1 lb (500 g) blade roast

1 lb (500 g) beef short ribs

1 lb (500 g) oxtails

1 lb (500 g) veal shanks

1 lb (500 g) lamb neck (with bones)

20–24 cups (5–6 L) cold water

2 medium carrots, halved

3 onions, halved

6 whole cloves

Bouquet garni—parsley sprigs, thyme, leek greens, and celery stalk

1–2 Tbsp (15–30 mL) coarse sea salt

10 whole peppercorns, tied in cheesecloth

2 cloves garlic, crushed

One 4–5-lb (2–2.5-kg) chicken, cut into about 12 pieces

This recipe's method might seem daunting, but if you have all of your ingredients ready, it's quite easy to make. A special shopping trip is called for. To make sure your list is complete, I've added a shopping list with the ingredients organized as you'd find them in the store. Before you serve the pot-au-feu, remove some of the cooking stock, add vermicelli to it, and serve it as a soup course. To accompany this dish, serve pickled vegetables, Dijon mustard, cornichons, horseradish, and sea salt in ramekins. Above all, don't forget the wine.

COVER THE BOTTOM OF A VERY LARGE POT (I suggest a large roasting pan covering two elements of your stove). Place the beef bones on the bottom as a rack. Place the beef shanks, blade roast, short ribs, and oxtails over the bones (the meat should not touch the bottom). Add the veal shanks and lamb neck last. Add cold water to cover all the meat. Don't add salt. Bring to a boil but do not cover (to avoid clouding the broth). Simmer over medium heat for about 20 minutes, then skim the fat from the surface with a spoon (if you tilt the pot, the fat will gather in one spot). Reduce to low-medium heat and simmer 20 minutes more.

Meanwhile, for the stock vegetables, turn on the oven broiler. Place the halved carrots and 1 halved onion in a broiling pan and grill the vegetables until blackened (this way, the vegetables will darken the broth). Stud the remaining onion halves with cloves and set aside. Make the bouquet garni by tying the herbs and greens together with a string.

After the meat has simmered for the second 20 minutes, skim the surface of the broth again. Add 2 tsp (10 mL) of coarse salt per 4 cups (1 L) of liquid. Add the bag of peppercorns, the garlic, blackened onions and carrots, clove-studded onion halves, bouquet garni, and chicken pieces. Arrange all the remaining vegetables (except tomatoes) on top of the meat in the order they are listed so that you can remove each type of vegetable as it is done. Skim again. Simmer slowly for about 40 minutes, skimming off the foam occasionally.

Remove the parsnip after 15 minutes and set aside in a large pot. With a slotted spoon, remove all the vegetables gently as they're cooked through (the vegetables are done when the point of a knife goes through) and transfer to the same pot. Pour about 2 ladles of broth over the vegetables and set aside. After 40 minutes, remove the chicken pieces, coat with a bit of broth, and keep warm.

Cook the meat for another 30 minutes, skimming the surface a few times. Remove the veal shanks and the lamb neck and keep covered along with the chicken. Cook the remaining meat gently for another hour.

While the meat is simmering, boil the vermicelli (if using), drain, rinse, and set aside in enough water to prevent the strands from sticking. Seal both ends of the marrow bones with carrot slices and tie them on with strings (this will keep the marrow in the bone). Cut the tomatoes, drain, chop, and set aside.

After an hour, tie the rump steak to the handles of the pot with string and let it hang in the liquid without touching the other meats. Add the marrow bones and the tomatoes. Skim one more time and let simmer for 10 to 15 minutes, according to the thickness of the rump steak.

Remove all the meats and marrow bones (discard the carrots and strings) and set aside. Return the vegetables, chicken, and reserved meats to the broth to warm up.

Arrange the meat on a large shallow serving platter with the beef shanks in the centre. Surround with the vegetables, chicken, reserved meats, and marrow bones and spoon some of the broth over.

If you're using the vermicelli, add it to the remaining broth and serve from a soup tureen. The broth can also be served with toasted bread and shredded cheese. It's traditional to add a couple of spoonfuls of red wine to the broth. Then bring out the platter of meat and vegetables and serve with the condiments.

SUGGESTED WINES
Beaujolais Pisse Dru, France
or Proprietor's Red, Cedar Creek, BC

30 baby carrots

20 peeled baby white turnips, or about twenty 2 x ½-inch (5 x 1-cm) sticks

3 medium leek whites, tied together with string

2 small celery roots (celeriac), sliced

5 Yukon Gold potatoes, peeled and sliced thickly

3 parsnips, peeled and cut into large sticks

5 beef marrow bones 1-inch (2.5-cm) thick

1 large carrot, sliced

3 large tomatoes

vermicelli (optional)

1 lb (500 g) tip of rump steak

A few spoonfuls red wine

Preparation time: 1 ½ hours
Cooking time: 3 to 3 ½ hours
Serves 8 to 10

Shopping List

Pot-au-feu

½ lb (250 g) beef bones
3 lb (1.5 kg) beef shanks
1 lb (500 g) blade roast
1 lb (500 g) beef short ribs
1 lb (500g) oxtails
1 lb (500 g) tip rump steak
1 lb (500 g) veal shanks
1 lb (500 g) lamb neck
    (with bones)
5 beef marrow bones
    1-inch (2.5-cm) thick
One 4–5-lb (2–2.5-kg) chicken,
    cut into about 12 pieces

2 medium carrots
1 large carrot
30 baby carrots
3 onions
3 leeks
1 stalk celery
2 small celery roots
20 baby white turnips
3 parsnips
5 Yukon gold potatoes
3 large tomatoes
Garlic
Flat-leaf parsley
Fresh thyme
Coarse sea salt
Whole peppercorns
Whole cloves
Vermicelli (optional)

All the flavours of Auvergne are on your plate with this dish. The potatoes, ham, pinch of garlic, and Saint-Nectaire come together in perfect harmony. Saint-Nectaire is a semisoft cow cheese similar to Reblochon. This is a great recipe if you want to do a simple, one-dish dinner meal. Just serve a frisée (chicory) salad on the side.

Saint-Nectaire Potato Cake

GÂTEAU DE POMMES DE TERRE AU SAINT-NECTAIRE

4 large Yukon Gold potatoes, cut into ¼-inch (5-mm) slices

4 cups (1 L) whipping cream

2 sprigs thyme

2 bay leaves

6 cloves garlic, halved

Salt and pepper

⅔ lb (350 g) Saint-Nectaire cheese (fine cheese shops)

2 frozen puff pastry sheets (thaw according to package instructions)

8 slices cooked ham

1 egg yolk beaten with 1 tsp (5 mL) water

Preparation time: 30 minutes
Cooking time: 40 minutes
Serves 6

PLACE THE POTATO slices in a saucepan and add the cream, thyme, bay leaves, and garlic. Bring to a boil and cook over medium heat for 20 to 25 minutes until tender. Season with salt and pepper. Drain, reserving the cream.

Preheat the oven to 425°F (220°C).

Remove the rind and thinly slice the cheese. Spread the puff pastry sheets on a floured surface and stretch enough with a rolling pin to form 2 round 14-inch (35-cm) sheets. Spread one sheet of dough onto an 11-inch (28-cm) pie pan. Spread half of the potatoes on top and garnish with ham and cheese. Cover with remaining potatoes and the reserved cream. Put the second puff pastry sheet on top. Roll the edges together to seal the pie. Prick the pastry with a fork and brush the egg yolk over the surface. Cook in the preheated oven for 15 minutes until the pastry has risen and is golden.

Remove from the oven and let it rest for 5 minutes before serving. Serve warm from the pie plate or transfer onto a serving plate.

SUGGESTED WINES
Côtes d'Auvergne, Madame Raymond Romeuf, France
or Gamay Noir, Mt. Boucherie, BC

This is an old recipe from the Rouergue, a region south of Auvergne. The recipe doesn't call for garlic, but you can rub the terrine with garlic or use chopped garlic in the dish; this is a matter of taste. The most important thing to remember is to beat the mixture constantly until it has the right texture, keeping the temperature low. If it's too warm, the cheese won't stretch and form threads. This potato dish is great served with pork sausages.

Potato and Cheese Purée

L' ALIGOT

8 large Yukon Gold potatoes, skin on

1 lb (500 g) fresh Tomme cheese, like Laguiole or Cantal (fine cheese shops)

½ cup (125 mL) unsalted butter

1 cup (250 mL) whipping cream

Salt and freshly ground pepper

Preparation time: 40 minutes
Cooking time: 40 minutes
Serves 6

SCRUB THE POTATO SKINS under cold water and place the whole potatoes in a large pot. Cover with cold water, bring to a boil, and cook for 30 minutes, depending on the size and quality. Drain and set aside to cool just enough so that you can handle them.

Thinly slice the cheese and set aside. Peel the potatoes and purée with a vegetable mill or mash with a potato masher in a bowl. Stir in the butter and cream and season with salt and pepper.

Transfer the mashed potatoes into a medium pot and heat slowly at low heat, while mixing with a wooden spoon. Incorporate the cheese, stirring vigorously. Continue to stir until threads form when the centre of the purée is lifted with a wooden spoon. Remove from the heat and serve immediately.

SUGGESTED WINES
Crozes Hermitage "Les Brunnelles," Caves des Papes, France
or Two, Sandhill, BC

The smooth sensation of warm, melting rice cake wrapped in unctuous sweet caramel on the palate brings back childhood memories. This is for the real sensuous gourmand in you!

Caramel Rice Pudding Cake

GÂTEAU DE RIZ AU CARAMEL

Milk Rice

3 ⅔ cups (900 mL) milk

⅓ cup (70 g) sugar

Pinch of salt

Vanilla bean,
cut in half lengthwise

1 cup (250 mL) long-grain white rice

¼ cup (60 mL) unsalted butter

3 egg yolks

Rice Pudding Cake

Cooked milk rice
(enough to fill up ⅔ of your mould)

3 eggs, separated

1¼ cups (310 mL) powdered sugar

Pinch of salt

½ cup (125 mL) sugar

Juice of ½ lemon

Preparation: 50 minutes
Cooking time: 45 minutes
Serves 4 to 6

MILK RICE

IN A MEDIUM PAN, slowly bring milk to a boil with split vanilla beans and sugar. In another pot, bring 4 cups (1 L) of water to a boil. Wash and drain rice, then pour into the boiling water. Cook for 2 minutes, drain well and transfer to the boiling milk. Reduce heat and let the rice simmer, uncovered, for 30 to 40 minutes, until cooked through and tender. Remove from heat. Remove the vanilla halves, add butter, and mix in the egg yolks one at a time.

NOTE: FOR ANOTHER TIME, AT THIS STAGE, YOU CAN SIMPLY SERVE MILK RICE LUKEWARM OR COLD WITH CRÈME ANGLAISE (SEE PAGE 141), OR A BERRY COULIS (SEE PAGE 141).

RICE PUDDING CAKE

Preheat the oven to 400°F (200°C).

In a bowl, mix the milk rice with the egg yolks and powdered sugar until well combined. Set aside. In another bowl, beat the egg whites with a pinch of salt until stiff peaks form. With a spatula, fold the meringue into the milk rice a little at a time.

In a small pot, mix the sugar, lemon juice and 1 Tbsp (15 mL) water. Bring to a boil and cook on medium heat until a soft caramel is formed. Pour half of the hot caramel into an 8-inch (20-cm) charlotte mould, swirling it around to coat the entire mould. Repeat with the remaining half of the caramel.

Pour the milk rice into the charlotte mould and place it in a shallow dish with water coming halfway up the sides. Place the bain-marie in the oven and cook for 45 minutes. Let cool and unmould onto a serving plate. Thin out the leftover caramel in the mould with hot water, and coat the rice pudding cake.

SUGGESTED WINES
Cap-Corse Muscatellu (muscat)
by Jean Noël Luigi, Clos Necrosi, Corsica
or Delice Late Harvest Muscat, Lake Breeze, BC

CARAMEL RICE PUDDING CAKE
PAGE 128

BAKED FRENCH ONION SOUP
PAGE 102

ESCARGOTS AND TOMATO CONFIT BAKE

PAGE 107

CHOCOLATE TARTS
PAGE 129

♦

The first thing to do when making this recipe is buy very good quality chocolate, like Valhrona Le Guanaja 70%. To the true chocolate lover, savouring chocolate as it slowly melts in the mouth is little short of orgasmic ... Are you ready for this?

Chocolate Tarts

TARTELETTES AU CHOCOLAT

Pastry

1 cup (250 mL) unsalted butter

½ cup (125 mL) icing sugar

1 ⅓ cups (330 mL) ground almonds

1 egg

2 cups (500 mL) all-purpose flour

Chocolate Filling

5 eggs

1 ¼ cups (310 mL) sugar

½ lb (250 g) chocolate
(refer to my note above)

1 ¼ cups (310 mL) unsalted butter

The day before: prepare the pastry dough
Preparation time: 15 minutes
Cooking time: 10 minutes
Serves 10

PASTRY

THE DAY BEFORE SERVING, prepare the pastry. In a bowl, cream the butter with a wooden spoon. Add the icing sugar, ground almonds, and egg, mixing well. When the ingredients are homogenous, incorporate the flour gradually, mixing well. Shape the dough into a ball, cover with plastic wrap, and refrigerate overnight.

CHOCOLATE FILLING

The next day, whisk the eggs and sugar with a hand-held mixer until the mixture whitens and doubles its volume. Melt the chocolate and butter in a double boiler over simmering water. Fold the warm chocolate into the egg mixture with a spatula. Transfer into a clean bowl, cover with plastic wrap, and chill completely.

continues on next page

To assemble

With a rolling pin, roll enough dough to line ten 2-inch (10-cm) greased tart shells (you can freeze the remaining dough for later use). Cut ten 4½-inch (11-cm) circles from the dough and insert into the tart shells. Rest the pastry for about 10 minutes in the refrigerator.

Preheat the oven to 300°F (150°C).

Make pie weights by wrapping dried lentils or beans in foil packages the same size as the moulds. Place the pie weights in the moulds and bake the tart shells in the preheated oven until they reach a light golden colour. Remove the pie weights, take the shells out of the moulds, and let cool.

When ready to serve, preheat the oven to 300°F (150°C). Spoon the chocolate filling into the cold shells and bake for 5 to 10 minutes, until the chocolate filling is warm and runny (the chocolate will run into the plate when the tart is cut with a fork.) Accompany with a splash of crème anglaise (see page 141). Serve with a spoon and a fork.

Suggested wines
Rasteau Rouge Mouelleux, Andrè Romero, France
or Summit Reserve Merlot Ice Wine, Mt. Boucherie, BC

No comments are necessary to describe this dessert. "Vive le chocolat!"

Chocolate Cake Régalade

GÂTEAU AU CHOCOLAT DE LA RÉGALADE

4 cups (1 L) strong coffee (espresso)

⅓ cup (80 mL) white rum

2 cups (500 mL) water

2 lb (1 kg) sugar (for pulled sugar)

2 oranges

10½ oz (300 g) chocolate
(Valhrona Le Guanaja 70% is what I use)

2 eggs

6 egg yolks

1¼ cups (300 mL) whipping cream

30 ladyfingers

Icing

10½ oz (300 g) chocolate

1¼ cups (310 mL) whipping cream

3 Tbsp + 1 tsp (50 mL) water

2 Tbsp (30 mL) honey

Preparation time: 1 ½ hours
Refrigeration time: 6 to 8 hours,
+ 2 hours
Serves 8

PREPARE THE STRONG COFFEE, sweeten with a bit of sugar, and add the white rum. Let cool.

Prepare the pulled sugar. In a large saucepan, mix the water with the sugar. Cook the sugar until it reaches 225°F (104°C) on a candy thermometer. Another way to verify when the pulled sugar is done is to wet your thumb and index finger with ice cold water, take a little bit of syrup, and pull the sugar until you see sugar threads between your fingers. Set the syrup aside.

Zest the 2 oranges. Soften the chocolate in a double boiler or a microwave oven. Set aside. Whisk the eggs and egg yolks together and incorporate into the pulled sugar. Whisk together until the pulled sugar and egg mixture is cold. Add the softened chocolate, zest, and cream. Mix well.

Grease an 8 x 10-inch (20 x 24-cm) rectangular mould. Soak the ladyfingers in the coffee and place half of them at the bottom of the mould. Fill in with the chocolate mixture and top with the other half of the soaked ladyfingers. Refrigerate for 6 to 8 hours. To slide the cake out of the mould, dip the sides and bottom of the mould into hot water before inverting the cake onto a cooling rack set over a pan.

ICING

Finely chop the chocolate and put in a large bowl. In a saucepan, bring the cream, water, and honey to a boil. Mix well before pouring the hot liquid onto the chopped chocolate. Stir with a spoon, and then glaze the cake with a spatula. Recover the glaze that has dripped into the pan and spread again. Transfer the cake to a serving dish and refrigerate for 2 hours. Serve very cold.

SUGGESTED WINES
Rivesaltes Red, Jean Michel Cazes, France
or Fortified Vintage Foch, Quails' Gate, BC

We attribute the origin of this dish's name, "Baba," to the king of Poland, Stanislas Leszczynski. He read the stories of A Thousand and One Nights *so often that he named this gourmet dessert after his favourite hero, Ali Baba.*

Rum Babas

BABAS AU RHUM

Babas

¾ cup (180 mL) unsalted butter

1 organic lemon

1⅓ cups (330 mL) all-purpose flour

1 Tbsp (15 mL) honey

1 Tbsp (15 mL) active dried yeast

1½ tsp (7 mL) salt

1 vanilla bean,
seeds only

8 eggs

Butter to grease moulds

NOTE: START PREPARING THIS RECIPE TWO DAYS IN ADVANCE, LETTING THE BABAS REST FOR 48 HOURS. YOU CAN FIND BABA MOULDS AT FINE COOKSHOPS, BUT YOU CAN ALSO USE MUFFIN TINS.

BABAS

CUT THE BUTTER into small cubes and leave at room temperature. Zest the lemon. In the bowl of a mixer, or in a food processor with a plastic blade, combine the flour, honey, yeast, salt, vanilla seeds, lemon zest, and 3 whole eggs. Knead the mixture in the mixer until the dough no longer sticks to the sides of the bowl. Add 3 more eggs to the dough and continue kneading at medium speed until the dough clears from the sides of the container once again. When done, add the 2 remaining eggs and continue kneading the dough for 10 minutes, adding the cubes of butter a few at a time until well incorporated.

Once the dough is smooth and liquid, transfer into a larger bowl, cover with plastic wrap, and let rest for 30 minutes at room temperature until the dough doubles in volume. Melt a bit of butter and brush the baba moulds. Half-fill the moulds with dough and let it rise to the top, about 30 minutes.

Preheat the oven to 400°F (200°C).

Bake the babas for 15 to 20 minutes until golden brown. Remove from the oven and let cool before inverting onto a cooling rack over a pan. Allow the babas to dry for 1 or 2 days—this makes them more absorbent! If you are keeping the babas longer than 2 days, store them in an airtight container.

Rum Syrup

1 organic orange

1 organic lemon

4 cups (1 L) cold water

3½ cups (875 mL) sugar

1 vanilla bean, split lengthwise

⅓ cup (80 mL) dark rum

Glaze

½ cup (125 mL) apricot jelly

¾ cup (180 mL) dark rum
(or more if you desire!)

Preparation time: 25 minutes
Rest: 2 days
Cooking time: 15 to 20 minutes
Yields 7 to 8 babas

RUM SYRUP

Zest the orange and lemon. In a saucepan, combine the water, sugar, and zest. Scrape the vanilla seeds into the pot, add the vanilla pod halves, and bring to a low boil, stirring to dissolve the sugar. Remove from the heat and add the rum. Insert a candy thermometer in the syrup and allow it to cool to 150° to 180°F (65° to 80°C). Soak the babas in the warm syrup for about 10 minutes. When the babas are soaked through they should have a spongelike consistency and not offer any resistance to a knife.

GLAZE

In a saucepan, bring the apricot jelly to a boil. With a pastry brush, moisten the babas with as much rum as you want and coat them with the hot apricot jelly. Garnish the rum babas with whipped cream and serve with a fruit salad if desired.

SUGGESTED WINES
Rivesaltes Domaine Frères Cazes, France
or Sequentia, Black Hills, BC

Madeleines

MADELEINES

1½ cups (375 mL) unsalted butter

1 cup (250 mL) sugar

1¾ cups (430 mL) all-purpose flour

1 tsp (5 mL) baking powder

4 whole eggs

3 Tbsp (45 mL) liquid honey

½ cup (125 mL) milk

Butter and flour for mould

Preparation time: 20 minutes
Cooking time: 10 to 15 minutes
Makes about a dozen

You don't need a special occasion to eat these delicious treats. They are ideal with coffee after dinner, or to accompany a dessert such as Floating Islands (see page 44) or Rhubarb and Apple Compote (see page 97). They keep well for up to a week in an airtight container. For a change, place a small piece of fruit on top of each madeleine before baking. The shell-shaped madeleine moulds can be found in fine cookshops.

IN A SAUCEPAN, melt and brown the butter at high heat. (It is the golden brown colour of the butter that will give the grilled flavour to the madeleines.) Remove from the heat and allow to cool completely.

Preheat the oven to 400 F° (200°C).

In a bowl, mix together the sugar, flour, and baking powder. In another bowl, beat the eggs, honey, and milk. Incorporate this mixture into the flour mixture. When the dough is smooth, add the cooled melted butter. (If the butter is hot or warm the madeleines will not rise.)

Butter and flour the madeleine mould and turn upside down to remove excess flour. Pour a heaping teaspoon of dough in each madeleine cup. Bake for 8 to 10 minutes or until golden brown. Remove from the oven and turn upside down on a wire rack. Cool with the rounded side up.

SUGGESTED BEVERAGE
Espresso, J.J. Beans Coffee, BC

134

Creampuffs
CHOUX À LA CRÈME

Choux Pastry

1 cup (250 mL) milk

1 cup (250 mL) water

1¼ cups (310 mL) unsalted butter

2 tsp (10 mL) salt

½ cup (125 mL) sugar

2¼ cups (560 mL) all-purpose flour

7 whole eggs

It's the contrast of textures that makes this French pastry so delicious. The cream is soft and rich and the caramel is sweet and crunchy. The kirsch is very important to the flavour, so don't omit it.

CHOUX PASTRY

POUR THE MILK AND WATER into a medium-sized pot. Add the butter, salt, and sugar and bring to a boil over medium heat. Remove from the heat and add the flour all at once, stirring constantly with a wooden spoon. Return to low heat and stir until the mixture does not stick to the sides of the pot.

Place the mixture in the mixer or in a food processor with a plastic blade and incorporate the whole eggs one at a time, mixing at high speed between additions. Transfer the dough into the refrigerator (it must be cold for the puffs to rise properly).

Preheat the oven to 450°F (230°C).

Lay wax or parchment paper out on a cookie sheet and hold the corners down with a small quantity of dough. If you have a pastry bag, fill it with the dough (no need for a tip). This will ensure an even shape for all of your puffs. If not, place tablespoon-sized balls of dough on the sheet, leaving 1 ½ inches (4 cm) in between.

Bake in the preheated oven for 10 minutes. After 10 minutes, lower the oven temperature to 300°F (150°C), turn the cookie sheet around so that the puffs are evenly cooked, and bake for 10 more minutes. Remove from the oven and cool completely.

CUSTARD

Pour the milk into a saucepan. Scrape the vanilla seeds out and set aside; add the empty pod halves to the milk. Bring to a soft boil and remove from the heat.

Combine the egg yolks, sugar, and vanilla seeds in a bowl and beat with a hand-held beater until the mixture whitens. With a wooden spoon, incorporate the flour into the egg mixture and mix well. Pour in the warm milk, stirring constantly.

Pour the mixture into a clean saucepan and place over low heat until it begins to boil. Remove from the heat once again. Remove the vanilla pod halves and pour in the kirsch. Spread a small slice of butter over the surface with a knife, to prevent the formation of a skin, and let stand to cool completely in the refrigerator.

CARAMEL

In a saucepan over medium heat, cook the sugar, water, and lemon juice. Remove from the heat as soon as the caramel is turning golden brown.

TO ASSEMBLE

Using a serrated knife, cut open the cold puffs near the base, leaving a hinge. Fit a pastry bag with a star tip and fill in the puffs with cold custard. Close the tops over the custard and dribble the caramel on top of the puffs. Serve on the same day.

SUGGESTED WINES
Sauternes, Château Coutet, France
or Late Harvest Chardonnay, Red Rooster, BC

Custard

2 cups (500 mL) milk

1 vanilla bean, split lengthwise

6 egg yolks

⅔ cup (160 mL) sugar

⅓ cup (80 mL) all-purpose flour

2 Tbsp (30 mL) kirsch

Butter

Caramel

6 Tbsp (90 mL) sugar

2 Tbsp (30 mL) water

A few drops lemon juice

Preparation time: 1 hour
Cooking time: 45 minutes
Serves 8

Other Recipes

BOUQUET GARNI

With kitchen string, tie together 5 to 6 fresh parsley stems (no leaves), 2 sprigs of fresh thyme, and 1 bay leaf. You can also tie them up in a cheesecloth bag for easy removal.

CLARIFIED BUTTER

Melt a slightly greater quantity of butter than the quantity required in the recipe. Skim off any foam and pour the clear liquid off the solids that collect on the bottom.

PESTO

3 cloves garlic, peeled and cut in two to remove centre sprout
2 bunches basil
3 Tbsp (45 mL) grated Parmesan
2 Tbsp (30 mL) pine nuts
⅔ cup (160 mL) extra virgin olive oil
Freshly ground black pepper and unrefined salt

Blend all the ingredients in a blender. This will keep well for a few days.

Tapenade Vinaigrette

½ cup (125 mL) pitted black olives
1 Tbsp (15 mL) capers
5 anchovy fillets
5 fresh basil leaves
1 clove garlic
1¼ cups (310 mL) olive oil
Salt and pepper

Pour all the ingredients into a food processor or a blender. Mix until you obtain a smooth vinaigrette.

Rice Pilaf

3 Tbsp (45 mL) unsalted butter
1 medium onion, finely chopped
2 cups (500 mL) basmati rice, rinsed and drained
1½ cups (375 mL) chicken stock
Bouquet garni (see page 138)

Preheat the oven to 400°F (200°C).

In a saucepan, melt 2 Tbsp (30 mL) of the butter and sweat the onion for 2 to 3 minutes. Add the rice and stir constantly with a wooden spoon. When the rice has absorbed the butter, add the chicken stock and bouquet garni. Bring to a boil, then pour into a greased 8-inch (2-L) casserole dish. Cover with a lid, or cut a piece of parchment paper to fit onto the casserole dish. Cook for 15 to 19 minutes without stirring. Taste with a fork to verify the doneness. Rest for a few minutes with the cover still on. Add the remaining 1 Tbsp (15 mL) butter and fluff the rice with a fork.

Macaroni Bake

2 cups (500 mL) macaroni
1 cup (250 mL) whipping cream
1½ cups (375 mL) milk
3 Tbsp (45 mL) unsalted butter
1 Tbsp (15 mL) all-purpose flour
Coarse salt, freshly ground pepper
¼ cup (60 mL) shredded Gruyère cheese

Bring a large pot of salted water to a boil with a bit of oil. Add the macaroni, bring back to a boil, stir with a wooden spoon, and cook for 3 minutes. Remove from the heat and leave in the hot water.

In a saucepan, bring the cream and milk to a boil over low heat. Remove from the heat and set aside.

Preheat the broiler.

In a heavy-bottomed pot, melt the butter. Add the flour and let cook a few minutes over medium heat, stirring with a spoon. Add the warm cream mixture, whisking constantly. Season with salt and pepper.

Drain the macaroni and rinse with cold water. Add the macaroni to the hot cream sauce and simmer for 4 minutes. Pour into a greased gratin dish, cover with the shredded Gruyère and bake until golden brown.

RED-BERRY COULIS

2 cups (500 mL) ripe red berries (strawberries or raspberries)
¼ cup (60 mL) sugar
1 Tbsp (15 mL) lemon juice (about ½ lemon)

Mix all the ingredients in a food processor or a blender. Strain though a fine sieve and discard the solids. Try using wild strawberries when in season!

CRÈME ANGLAISE

This party-sized recipe can easily be halved, but if you want to make even less, try the recipe on page 44.

2 vanilla beans
12 egg yolks
2 cups (500 mL) sugar
4 cups (1 L) milk

Crush the vanilla beans with a heavy knife and cut in two lengthwise. In a bowl, whisk the egg yolks and the sugar until the mixture whitens. In a large pot, bring the milk with the crushed vanilla pod halves to a boil, over low heat. Remove the pods and pour the boiling milk into the egg mixture, constantly whisking. Pour the custard back into the pot, and cook over very low heat, stirring with a wooden spoon, for about 5 minutes.

The custard is done when your finger leaves a clear line through it, coating a spoon. At that point, remove from the heat, strain through a sieve into a clean bowl, and place the bowl in a larger bowl of ice to stop the cooking. This will keep for up to 4 days in the refrigerator.

NAVETTE BREAD

3½ cups (950 mL) all-purpose flour
1 cup (250 mL) whole wheat flour
2 tsp (10 mL) salt
1 Tbsp (15 mL) fresh yeast
    (from a bakery or the dairy section of gourmet markets)
½ cup (125 mL) water

Pour the flours and salt into the bowl of a stand mixer with a kneading blade. In a small bowl, mix the yeast into the water. Add the yeast slurry to the dry ingredients and mix at medium speed, allowing the dough to knead. It's ready when the dough no longer sticks to the sides.

Roll the dough into a ball. With a knife, slash the surface and place the dough in a large, greased earthenware bowl covered with a damp cloth. Let the dough rise for 2 hours at room temperature.

Preheat the oven to 450°F (230°C).

Flour your hands, punch the dough, and fold it 4 times. Let the dough rise again and cover with a damp cloth.

Divide the dough in 3 pieces and shape into oval loaves, spacing them out on a baking sheet. Sprinkle with flour, cover with a dry cloth, and let them rise one more time until the loaves double their size. Slash parallel diagonal lines in the tops and bake for 20 to 30 minutes. Allow the loaves to rest for 12 hours before eating.

BC Wineries

ASOLO VINEYARDS
400–601 West Broadway
Vancouver, BC, V5Z 4C2
604-871-4329
www.asolo.ca

BLACK HILLS ESTATE WINERY
30880 Black Sage Road
Oliver, BC, V0H 1T0
250-498-0666
www.blackhillswinery.com

BLUE MOUNTAIN VINEYARD & CELLARS
RR1, S3, C4
Okanagan Falls, BC, V0H 1R0
250-497-8244
www.bluemountainwinery.com

BURROWING OWL ESTATE WINERY
100 Burrowing Owl Place (off Black Sage Road)
Oliver, BC, V0H 1T0
1-877-498-0620
www.bovwine.com

CEDARCREEK ESTATE WINERY
5445 Lakeside Road
Kelowna, BC, V1W 4S5
250-764-8866
www.cedarcreek.bc.ca

DOMAINE DE CHABERTON
1064–216th Street
Langley, BC, V2Z 1R3
604-530-1736
www.domainedechaberton.com

FAIRVIEW CELLARS
Old Golf Course Road (13147–334th Avenue)
Oliver, BC, V0H 1T0
250-498-2211

GEHRINGER BROTHERS ESTATE WINERY
Road 8
Oliver, BC, V0H 1T0
250-498-3537

GRAY MONK ESTATE WINERY
1055 Camp Road
Okanagan Centre, BC, V4V 2H4
250-766-3168
www.graymonk.com

HESTER CREEK ESTATE WINERY
13163–326th Avenue
Oliver, BC, V0H 1T0
250-498-4435
www.hestercreek.com

HILLSIDE ESTATE
1350 Naramata Road
Penticton, BC, V2A 8T6
250-493-6274
www.hillsideestate.com

JACKSON-TRIGGS VINTNERS & OSOYOOS LAROSE
38691 Highway 97 North
Oliver, BC, V0H 1T0
250-498-4981
www.atlaswine.com

LA FRENZ WINERY
740 Naramata Road
Penticton, BC, V2A 8T5
250-492-6690
www.lafrenzwinery.bc.ca

LAKE BREEZE VINEYARDS
930 Sammet Road
Naramata, BC, V0H 1N0
250-496-5659

MISSION HILL FAMILY ESTATE WINERY
1730 Mission Hill Road
Westbank, BC, V4T 2E4
250-768-7611
www.missionhillwinery.com

MT. BOUCHERIE ESTATE WINERY
829 Douglas Road
Kelowna, BC, V1Z 1N9
250-769-8803
www.mtboucherie.bc.ca

NICHOL VINEYARD & FARM WINERY
1285 Smethurst Road
Naramata, BC, V0H 1N0
250-496-5962

POPLAR GROVE WINERY
1060 Poplar Grove Road
Penticton, BC, V2A 8T6
250-492-2352
www.poplargrove.ca

QUAILS' GATE ESTATE WINERY
3303 Boucherie Road
Kelowna, BC, V1Z 2H3
250-769-4451
www.quailsgate.ca

RED ROOSTER WINERY
891 Naramata Road
Penticton, BC, V2A 8T5
250-492-2424
www.redroosterwinery.com

SANDHILL WINES
1125 Richter Street
Kelowna, BC, V1Y 2K6
1-888-246-4472
www.sandhillwines.ca

SATURNA ISLAND VINEYARDS & WINERY
8 Quarry Road
Saturna Island, BC, V0N 2Y0
250-539-5139
www.saturnavineyards.com

STAG'S HOLLOW WINERY
2237 Sun Valley Way
Okanagan Falls, BC, V0H 1R0
250-497-6162
www.stagshollowwinery.com

SUMAC RIDGE ESTATE WINERY
17403 Highway 97
Summerland, BC, V0H 1Z0
250-494-0451
www.sumacridge.com

TINHORN CREEK VINEYARDS
    32830 Tinhorn Creek Road
    Oliver, BC, V0H 1T0
    1-888-484-6467
    250-498-3743
    www.tinhorn.com

TOWNSHIP 7 VINEYARDS & WINERY
    21152–16th Avenue
    Langley, BC, V2Z 1K3
    604-532-1766
    www.township7.com

WILD GOOSE VINEYARDS
    2145 Sun Valley Way
    Okanagan Falls, BC, V0H 1R0
    250-497-8919
    www.wildgoosewinery.com

Index

152

About the Author

October 24, 1951. It was a gloomy day in Fontainebleau, an ancient French royal city that was home to many illustrious men, like François I, Louis XIV and little Napoleon. That was the day I was born. Mother once said that my culinary instincts were already acute, since I was born at high noon!

I lived a quiet childhood and was a good student who didn't get into too much trouble. I was 14 years old when my father passed away. The following year I left for Samois sur Seine, a small village on Fontainebleau's forest border, for my *apprentissage*, learning my culinary skills and funnelling my passions. After three years of hard labour, earning my toque and a national mention, I left for Paris and worked in different establishments as a third cook. Spending a season working at St. Maxime on the French Riviera, I discovered the good life!

After more time in Paris, I came to Vancouver in 1972, where I enjoyed the laid-back attitude and friendliness of the people on Canada's West Coast. I worked at the Panorama Roof of the Hotel Vancouver with Jean-Claude Ramond. Returning to France in 1975, I moved to Albertville, the Olympic city, where I owned my first restaurant and earned a Michelin star. My elder son, Olivier, was born in 1978, followed by Steeve in 1981. Steeve works with me and is a great part of La Régalade.

After selling the restaurant in Albertville in 1985, I came back to Paris on Rue du Colisée and owned a restaurant named Alain Rayé, offering innovative French fine cuisine. In March of 1986, I met my wife, Brigitte. She gave birth to Kevin in 1989. In 1992, after a successful seven-year operation, the family moved to Châteaufort, a village in the Vallée de Chevreuse, where we bought the restaurant La Belle Époque, and once again earned a Michelin star. Inspired by the dishes of the restaurant, I wrote my first cookbook *Une table pour deux*, pairing recipes with the artistry of my great friend and painter, Thierry Vaubourgoin.

In 1998, looking for different opportunities and a much-deserved break, the family spent some time in Boston, then moved to Vancouver in August 1999, reacquainting ourselves with this beautiful city. La Régalade opened its doors in West Vancouver in February of 2001. Four years later, I'm proud to present to you my second cookbook, based on the bistro dishes offered at La Régalade.

More culinary adventures in my next book...